VAMPIRES

VAMPIRES

The Myths, Legends, and Lore

CHARLOTTE MONTAGUE

CHARTWELL
BOOKS

Contents

Contents

Introduction

The legend of the vampire has never been more popular than it is today. Millions of copies of Stephenie Meyer's *Twilight* series have been sold, and the vampire continues to be represented in many imaginative forms on stage and screen, whether in the theatre, in film, on TV, or in the field of popular music. On the internet, entire websites are devoted to the cult of the vampire, discussing details of lifestyle, dress and beliefs. In most cases, this fascination with the myth is harmless enough: it is simply a playful and enjoyable way for us to address some of our most confusing and difficult experiences in life, such as our fear of death, our longing for immortality, and our mixed feelings about becoming sexual beings as we grow up. However, there are instances in which the figure of the vampire attracts those with more evil intent, or those who suffer from various forms of mental illness. These are the individuals who take the legend literally, and begin to act accordingly: the devotees, past or present, known and feared for their bloodthirsty ways or their bizarre ritual practices.

Bela Lugosi as Dracula in the 1930 film classic

In this book, we will be looking at all of these manifestations of the vampire myth, from its genesis in folklore to its status today as one of the most iconic figures in popular culture. We will try to find out how this strange creature, who came into being centuries ago as a minor figure in an obscure pagan belief system, that of the 'old religion' of the Slavic countries, eventually managed to dominate the gothic imagination of the Victorians and beyond, in the process transforming itself from a hideous monster into the suave villain we know today.

The origins of the vampire legend go back centuries, to the dark forests of Transylvania, and the pagan beliefs of the Slavic peoples. They are shrouded in mystery, since the religious practices of these peoples were not written down, but we know that vampire folklore dominated the lives of rural peasants and priests during the Middle Ages. In particular, these communities were concerned with death and disease. At a time when medicine was in its infancy, and superstition was rife, the idea of the revenant, coming back from the grave to wreak revenge on the living, was highly potent, and struck deep fear into the largely uneducated population of the time.

Although Christianity had been introduced into these countries, peasant folk still retained their pagan beliefs. Among these was the idea that after death, the souls of those who had suffered in life, or who had committed crimes, were condemned to wander the earth for ever, alone and shunned by human society. This exclusion from love, and life, was thought to give the dead a deep resentment of the living, causing their spirits to rise from the grave as vampires. It was believed that these malign beings would make their way to villages and towns, bringing with them plagues and fatal diseases from the grave.

In the medieval imagination, the vampire was a vile, corpse-like being, swollen with blood and with its flesh rotting, whose revolting smell brought a foul pestilence into the streets where it walked at night, looking for victims. Today, this notion of the vampire as a lonely, reviled figure continues to be part of the myth. Other aspects of the medieval myth, such as the idea of the vampire as a bringer of plague from the dead, have become less important. This is perhaps because we now have access to medical science, and the process whereby the human body decomposes after death is better understood. The characteristics that so frightened the medieval peasant, such as bloating and swelling of the body, with fresh blood running out of the orifices, have been scientifically explained. In addition, the ways in which communicable diseases are spread are better understood, so that most of us no longer believe, when an epidemic breaks out, that a vampire may be responsible.

Over the centuries, the vampire myth originating from the Slavic countries began to spread throughout Europe, fuelled by tales of vampire sightings. In some cases, government officials were sent to quell panic in a remote area, only to come back with accounts of priests opening up graves to find bodies that had swelled and grown fat, with ruddy cheeks and blood running from their mouths, their hair and fingernails grown long while they sojourned underground. These sensational stories were reported in the newspapers, thrilling and horrifying the general population. In this way, the more literate classes of the eighteenth century began to become fascinated by vampires, and by the nineteenth, they had made their way into literature and art.

The vampire legend particularly appealed to the gothic taste of the Victorians, who revelled in tales of gloomy castles, northern forests, and evil ghouls lying in wait for innocent travellers. In this period, the most famous vampire of them all, Count Dracula, was born. He was the brainchild of Bram Stoker, whose refined, aristocratic bloodsucker caught the public imagination. Some cultural historians have argued that the figure of Dracula was a metaphor for the parasitic existence of the upper classes, and their dependence on poverty-stricken and brutally treated lower orders. Whether or not this was the reason for the Count's popularity, Stoker's novel spawned a whole host of imitators, and in the twentieth century, went on to inspire new generations of artists, writers, and film-makers.

Today's vampire is a very different creature from the monster of the medieval imagination, or even the ghoulish aristocrat of Victorian horror stories. In modern novels and films, the status of the vampire as, on the surface, indistinguishable from 'normal' human beings, is emphasized. Vampires are also characterized as having human emotions, that is, falling in love, feeling the pain of separation, loss, and vilification, and, most importantly, being anguished about their predicament as 'undead' beings from the grave, excluded from human society and responsible for corrupting the lovers and friends with whom they form attachments. In this way, the modern vampire myth speaks to our ambiguous feelings about individuals who are, traditionally, excluded in our society: for example, drug users, people with unusual sexual orientations and the mentally ill. It also resonates with deep-seated fears, especially among young people, that passionate sexual feelings may arouse violence, and do harm to those we love.

In modern times, the vampire myth continues to be a powerful metaphor for sexual initiation, expressing fears and desires about sexual experience as part of

the process of growing up. It appeals in particular to teenage girls, who now devour vampire books and films with enormous enthusiasm. There are differing arguments as to why this is so. Some psychologists have argued that the 'biting' aspect of the vampire myth is a form of infantile sexuality, brought into play in the teenage years so as to avoid the realities of sexual intercourse. Be that as it may, there is no doubt that the idea of the handsome young vampire (who is also hundreds of years old, and has several lifetimes' worth of experience) is an immensely attractive figure to many young women, as the tremendous success of the *Twilight* series, both in book and film form, attests.

But what of the vampire legend worldwide? The myth is not only present in European folklore, literature, and modern media, but is also found – in different forms – all over the world. In almost all cultures of the globe, revenant stories exist, and many of them involve the central element of the vampire myth, which is the drinking of blood. From earliest times, there have been stories of vampire-like creatures such as the blood-sucking Lamia of Ancient Greece, and Lilith, the seductive storm demon of Mesapotamia who brings disease and death. The Romans believed in the Strix, an evil nocturnal bird who fed on flesh like the vampire, while the Aztecs feared the Cihuateteo, the spirits of women who had died in childbirth, who haunted crossroads, eager to seize young children and carry them off. From Africa comes the Asanbosam, a vampire-like creature believed to have iron teeth and to live in trees, swooping down to attack its victims, and from the Philippines the Aswang, a female bat-like spirit who eats the dead and steals children.

There are also contemporary vampire stories in many parts of the developing world that, in some cases, have acquired the status of urban myths. Today, in Puerto Rico and Mexico, there are communities who still believe in the Chupacabra, the goat sucker, who attacks herds of livestock and drinks their blood. Sightings of this bizarre creature – said to be the size of a small bear, with a row of spines that run along its back from head to tail – have been reported in many different parts of the Americas. Whether they are true or false it is hard to say, but what is clear is that all these vampire myths bear witness to universal human anxieties: about death, about what happens to us after we die, and how the spirits of the departed, especially those who have experienced suffering or mistreatment, may return to haunt us.

Most of us see the vampire legend as an entertaining, perhaps somewhat disturbing, form of horror fiction. However, there are certain individuals, both historical and contemporary, for whom vampirism becomes a way of life. These are the people who take the myth to an extreme, killing to satisfy their lust for blood. In the past, people who showed violent, bloodthirsty, and often severely mentally ill behaviours might be thought of as vampires. Indeed, serial killers, as we would call them today, were quite often dubbed 'vampires' – for example, Peter Kürten, the serial killer known as 'The Vampire of Düsseldorf' who murdered and tortured children, and Richard Trenton Chase, who, after killing six people in California in 1977, was nicknamed 'The Vampire of Sacramento' because he drank his victims' blood and ate parts of their internal organs.

The forerunners of these serial killer 'vampires' are infamous historical figures such as Vlad the Impaler, Gilles de Rais, and Countess Elizabeth Báthory. These were the serial killers of their day, men and women who loved to kill for the perverse pleasure that horrific acts of cruelty gave them. What is most shocking about these killers is that they were powerful members of the ruling class, and therefore were allowed to kill hundreds of victims more or less with impunity. The most infamous of all, perhaps, is Vlad, who had a barbarous habit of skewering people on sharpened stakes, sometimes hundreds at a time, including infants and their mothers. Gilles de Rais, another brutal military man, was a Breton knight and companion of Joan of Arc who seems to have lost his mind and become a sadistic serial killer of children. In both these cases, the day-to-day killing of human beings on the field of combat seems to have sparked off a thirst for blood that could not be quenched. And finally, there is perhaps the most shocking case of all, the viciously insane Countess Elizabeth Báthory, who tortured and killed hundreds of young women in her remote Hungarian castle, and who has gone down in history as the most

prolific female serial killer of all time.

Real vampires, then, are anything but entertaining: they show us the dark side of the myth, and the horror that may ensue when deranged individuals take it literally and act upon it. By contrast, the vampires of imagination, in popular culture through the ages, have been a staple of the horror genre, providing an endless source of inspiration for poets, writers, film-makers, and artists. Beginning with the Romantics, we find the first vampires to make their appearance in English literature, in the works of such masters as John Keats, Samuel Taylor Coleridge, and Lord Byron, whose friend and physician John Polidori wrote the seminal story *The Vampyre*, published in 1819.

The Victorian vampire craze in literature continued with such figures as Varney the Vampire, the sympathetic hero of the 'penny dreadfuls', cheap serial editions of horror stories aimed at teenagers. Varney is one of the first 'sympathetic' literary vampires, described as essentially human, and to some degree, humane, but suffering from a horrible condition that compels him to seek blood from his victims to survive. This theme later becomes central to vampire literature, until in contemporary stories the figure of the vampire stands as a metaphor for an ordinary individual afflicted by destructive sexual drives that he or she cannot control, and that inspire self-loathing, guilt, and disgust. In this portrayal, we feel sympathy for the vampire, and are able to empathize with his or her condition.

There is an early forerunner of the lesbian vampire story in another Victorian classic, Sheridan Le Fanu's *Carmilla*, a tale of repressed desire between two young women that thrilled Victorian readers with its combination of gothic horror, forbidden romance, and sexual innuendo. We then encounter the greatest vampire novel of all

Nosferatu The Vampyre movie poster, 1979

time: Bram Stoker's *Dracula*, which brings together all these strands in a narrative of drama, passion, and power. We explore some of the profound themes of the novel, such as the conflict between belief in the rational (science, medicine, and technology) and the irrational (ancient folkloric beliefs in supernatural forces such as spirits, and demons). We also find out where Stoker got his inspiration for the story, and most importantly, how he created the character of the most famous vampire in literature, Count Dracula.

In the twentieth and twenty-first century, vampire fiction continues apace with novels such as Richard Matheson's *I Am Legend* in the 1950s, to Anne Rice's seminal *Vampire Chronicles* beginning in the 1970s, to today's massively popular *Twilight* series by Stephenie Meyer. In the cinema, too, the vampire becomes a staple of the horror genre, beginning with F.W. Murnau's cult classic *Nosferatu* in 1922, based on the Stoker novel, and continuing with such milestones as *Dracula* in 1931 starring Bela Lugosi, and the Hammer Horror series starring Christopher Lee, which commenced in 1958. We also visit the vampires of popular television, including Barnabas Collins of the ABC TV series *Dark Shadows* and Buffy Summers of *Buffy the Vampire Slayer*. The vampires of popular music are not forgotten, as we remember such iconic figures as Screamin' Jay Hawkins, who emerged from a smoke-filled coffin on stage, complete with cape and voodoo cane, and his musical progeny Alice Cooper, stalwart of the rock'n'roll horror genre, who introduced a further element of mayhem onto the stage with mock executions by electric chair, gallows, and guillotine. In the same vein is today's Marilyn Manson, who continues to wave the banner for heavy metal and tasteless gore, and whose antics are perennially censured by the authorities, in the finest rock tradition.

Today, it seems that our long love affair with the vampire, if it can be termed as such, looks set to continue. The vile monster from the grave that plagued the medieval imagination has, in the new millennium, been replaced by a more sympathetic, sensitive and humane character. Today, the vampire stands as a metaphor for the civilized, cultured human being who is still, at heart, prey to dark, irrational forces that he or she cannot always control. It is as if, in the figure of the vampire, the human race preserves a memory of our ancient pagan culture, and refuses to let go of it, recognizing its continuing power to express our ever-present primitive fears – and hopes – about the nature of life, death and immortality.

Twilight movie poster, 2008

CHAPTER I

The Rise of the Vampire Myth

any cultures around the world contain folkloric stories about human beings who die, are buried, and come back to life at night to visit loved ones. However, the particular, and often menacing, habits of the revenants that we find in stories of vampires are very specific to what is called the 'old religion' of the Slavs, in which the soul was believed to come back and haunt the living after death.

Domovoi, a spirit of the house

The 'old religion'

The Slavic 'old religion' pre-dates the Christianization of the Slavic countries by many years. It is a set of ancient pagan beliefs and rituals that continued to be held and practised well after Christianity was introduced in the region. Much of it was never written down, which is why the source of many of its rituals is unknown today. It centres on a number of beliefs about household spirits, some of which were considered benevolent, others which were thought of as evil. These spirits would be invoked to help with domestic and farming tasks, but they often refused to, and instead wreaked havoc and destruction. If there was bad weather at harvest time, or if accidents happened, the spirits would be blamed. In addition, there was a superstition that if a human or animal became ill, it might be explained by the presence of a spirit sucking their lifeblood away.

These often demonic spirits were, the Slavs believed, the spirits of ancestors who needed to be appeased. In pre-Christian Slavic culture, it was thought that when a person died, their soul would continue to live, and would haunt the farm, village, or town where they had spent their years on earth. This haunting might continue for a month or longer until the soul finally decided to leave the area and find rest. For this reason, families would leave a door or a window open so that the spirit could come in or out of the house at will. It was important for families to do everything they could to please the spirit, or the spirit might make their lives a complete misery.

In order to make sure that the spirit went its way as soon as possible without causing too much trouble, it was considered important that all burial rites should be carefully observed. If they were not, the soul of the departed might become 'unclean', and its spirit would then become malevolent. Inevitably, proper burial did not always take place: for example, if a baby or child died before it had been baptized, or if a person met a sudden or violent end, in an accident or a fight, and the body was not found in time to bury it before it decomposed. Moreover, if the person who died was a sinner – for example, a person who practised black magic, or someone who had committed a murder – his or her soul would not pass away peacefully, but might, it was believed, haunt the living for years to come. In the worst case, the unclean soul might become a vampire – that is, a wicked spirit in a decomposing body, who fed on the blood of the living.

A SPIRIT SUCKING THEIR LIFEBLOOD AWAY

River demons

The vampire was just one of a number of hellish spirits in Slavic mythology. For example, a Rusalka was a female, mermaid-like demon that lured men away from their wives and families. She might emerge from the water and sit singing songs in a tree, until she caught the attention of a labourer in the fields. In some myths, the Rusalka was beautiful, with long hair and luminous green eyes, while in others, she was ugly and covered in hair. She might take a man or child away to live with her on the riverbed, or appear as a Succubus, tempting a man to have sex with her over and over again, until he became utterly exhausted. In this way she would draw his life force out of him, and use it to sustain herself, in vengeance for a wrong that had been done to her in life. Whatever form she took, she was essentially an unquiet spirit who had died a violent death, for example committing suicide because of an unwanted pregnancy. The belief was that if the young woman's death was avenged, her spirit would be able to rest at last, and would stop harassing the living. In other myths, the Rusalka could be an unbaptized child born out of wedlock, whose mother had murdered it.

The male counterpart of the Rusalka is the Vodyanoy, a river creature who looked like a naked old man with a long, shabby beard and tangled wet hair. His body was covered in slime and black fish scales, and his hands were webbed. He had a tail like a fish, and burning red eyes. He rode about on a log, looking for people to drown, and when he succeeded, dragged them down to the bottom of the river to work for him as servants. When the captured victims died, the creature was believed to store their soul in special porcelain cups. Fishermen were in great awe of the Vodyanoy, whom they considered lord of the river, and made continual sacrifices to appease him.

House demons

Domestic gods in the Slavic pantheon included the Domovoi, and his female counterpart, the Kikimora. The Domovoi was a hairy little creature, sometimes with horns, who watched over a house. If the inhabitants behaved well, and left milk and biscuits out for him, the creature would help with the farm work and household chores. He could also predict the future, and might warn a family of impending danger by pulling the hair of the woman of the house, or tell of good news such as a wedding by making strumming noises on a comb. However, if the Domovoi was angered, it could break dishes, leave muddy footprints on the floor, or make moaning noises. When this happened, the family had to work out what was going wrong, and make amends. Significantly, in terms of the vampire myth, if he was really angered, he might make threats to stifle members

Illustration of Slavic mermaid, the Rusalka

of the family as they slept in their beds. However, if his needs were fulfilled, the family could live peacefully with him.

The Kikimora, another house spirit, was thought to be the female spirit of an unbaptized child. She appeared as a small, skinny witch with long unkempt hair, and sometimes a humpback. In some stories, she wore dirty clothes. When angered, the Kikimora was said to keep children awake at night, tickling them or whistling in their ears. At night, she would come out from her hiding place behind the stove and sit spinning. If any human being saw her at her work, they would be likely to die shortly afterwards.

'Double faith'

When the various Slavic populations began to be Christianized between the seventh and twelfth centuries, these old pagan beliefs did not die out. Among the rural peasantry, the 'old religion' continued to be observed, along with the new Christian rituals. The peasants took to Christianity with enthusiasm, adopting all the main rituals, particularly baptism, but continued to worship their ancient gods at the same time. This 'double faith', as it was

called, angered the authorities in Slavic countries, and Christian priests were employed to stamp it out, but to no avail. It seems that the Slavic peasants saw no contradiction between the two religions, and merely added a new set of Christian beliefs to their old pagan ones. As the centuries passed, these beliefs became intertwined, so that country people often saw themselves as devout Christians, while viewing the natural world, and their place in it, as ruled entirely by demons, sprites, and spirits.

What is significant about all this in terms of the vampire myth, is how often the notion of an evil revenant spirit, somehow wronged in life and returning to wreak vengeance on the living, comes up in pagan Slavic beliefs. These spirits are most commonly thought to be the restless souls of people who, in life, were sinned against or had sinned. Christian baptism and burial comes to feature prominently in this world view as a way of making amends for such wrongs. Where these rituals have not been properly observed, special measures are thought to be needed, and this is where the strange vampire-killing rites – exhuming corpses, staking, and so on – begin to develop.

By the eighteenth century, when Christian priests were beginning to perform these special measures, usually at the request of superstitious village communities, panic broke out as they observed the strangely lifelike appearance of decomposing corpses, and reported their findings to the authorities. For the first time, the pagan notions of evil sprites, demons, vampires, etc, previously dismissed as the foolish stories of ignorant peasants, began to have some credibility. And when these accounts were published in the newspapers, the panic began to spread, so that the public's faith in science and rationality, cornerstones of the Age of Enlightenment, was shaken to the core.

The etymology, or derivation, of the word 'vampire' mirrors the rise of superstitious beliefs in Europe from the Dark Ages onwards. Some of these beliefs date back to pagan times, and to ancient folklore in remote rural regions of the north; others are rooted in the most lurid kinds of medieval Christian imagery, particularly descriptions of hell, the devil, and all kinds of monstrous, evil demons. As is outlined below, such folkloric stories, superstitions and taboos often arose as a way of explaining everyday phenomena that peasants would have witnessed at close hand. These would have included the behaviour of blood-drinking animals such as bats and wolves; the strange and often highly alarming way that human bodies decompose after death; and blood-related features of communicable diseases, ranging from plagues to tuberculosis to porphyria. Such superstitions were based in ignorance and fear; they were, for the most part, stories told by uneducated peasant communities about the frightening, cruel, and brutal conditions of life around them, and which they had little scientific knowledge about. However, these stories also expressed some deep-rooted, and understandable, anxieties about a world in which their needs, their individual circumstances, and their common humanity was often ignored. For that reason, these stories are still powerful today.

The first 'wicked vampire'

The word 'vampire', in its written form, first appeared in the eleventh century as a scribbled note in a manuscript of the Book of Psalms. This was translated by a humble priest for a Novgorodian prince, Vladimir Yaroslavovich. In the note, the priest addresses the prince as 'upir lichyj' (a 'wicked vampire'). Whether this was a joke, a nickname, or a serious criticism (which is unlikely, given the power of the prince and the lowly position of the priest), is unknown. We next find the word in a treatise called *The Word of Saint Grigoriy*, which reported the existence of pagan rituals in Russia, and fulminated against them in no uncertain terms. No one knows exactly when this evangelical Christian treatise was written, but it seems to have been prior to the fourteenth century, when the church was keen to stamp out the pagan beliefs and rituals of ordinary working people, especially in remote rural areas of northern Europe.

Pagan worship of non-Christian deities and devils was known to be rife in the Slavic countries of Europe throughout the medieval period, but the word 'vampire' does not actually appear in print in England until the mid-eighteenth century. We first come across it when it is mentioned in a travelogue entitled, *The Travels of Three English Gentlemen from Venice to Hamburg, being the Grand Tour of Germany, in the Year 1734*. Little is said in the text about the actual vampire in question itself, but the fact that it is alluded to makes it clear that belief in such evil demons was becoming more widespread across the countries of Europe during this time.

We know for a fact from historical records that after Austria gained control of parts of Serbia and Romania in 1918, officials complained about the local practice of exhuming corpses to kill off 'vampire' spirits. The officials prepared detailed reports on these gruesome rituals, which were widely publicized at the time and enthusiastically received – as they are today – by a public with a seemingly insatiable appetite for horror and gore.

The word 'vampire'

Theories about the derivation of the word 'vampire' in English vary, but it appears to have been borrowed from the German word 'vampir', which in turn came from the Polish 'vaper'. There are parallel words for vampire, ranging from 'vapir' to 'upir', in almost all the Slavic languages, including Bulgarian, Croatian, Czech, Slovak, Polish, Russian, and Ukrainian. The general etymology of the word is somewhat controversial and uncertain, but it is thought to have links to the word for bat in Russian (netopyr), witch in Turkic (ubyr), and from various Indo-European words for the verb to fly.

Today, the word vampire is defined variously as 'a corpse that rises nightly from its grave to drink the blood of the living' and 'a mythical creature which overcomes death by sucking the blood from living humans'. Some dictionaries and reference works note that portraying the vampire as a corpse in a grave who comes out at night to seek victims, especially those sleeping in their beds, is only one variation of the myth. Other features of vampire lore, such as the creature's ability to fly, its fear of Christian symbols like the cross, and its susceptibility to sunlight, have been added over the years. The myth has also been elaborated on in other ways, for example in numerous apotropaics – that is, items (such as garlic) or methods (such as driving a stake through the heart) designed to kill the vampire.

Vampirism & Corpses

It is hard to understand why the myth of the vampire arose in Western culture, until we look at the context in which these stories and beliefs came to be. When we do, we find that the idea of the vampire came about largely as a result of fears and misunderstandings about the nature of death and the decomposition of the human corpse. In medieval times, it was common for ordinary people to see human bodies after they had died; partly, because poor peasants had to bury their own dead, but also because religious rituals often involved leaving an open coffin in the house for relatives and friends to pay their respects. Some modern-day commentators believe that this tradition, odd as it may seem to us today, was in fact psychologically quite healthy; in order to accept that a loved one has truly departed, the family need to see the dead body and acknowledge that the person is no longer a living being.

However, there were also negative aspects to this natural cycle. Human corpses sometimes decompose in a particularly horrifying way, according to the cause of death (liver complaints, for instance, might turn a body green), and the particular conditions in which the body is being stored (excess heat, excess cold, damp, and so on). In societies where little was known about medicine or science, and where irrational beliefs in demons, evil spirits, and so on were rife, it was easy for onlookers to imagine that a dead body had been taken over by such spirits, and that consequently it was a source of danger.

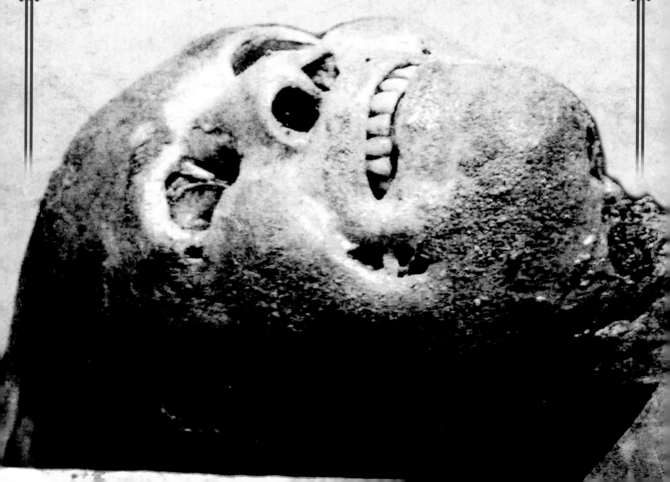

Exhumation of bodies

In cases where bodies were exhumed because they were suspected of being vampires, there could be changes in its appearance that would cause extreme fear and consternation. In certain conditions, depending on the temperature of the soil and its composition, corpses can release gases as they decompose, and these can sometimes cause the body to swell up. In addition, blood may run to the skin, causing it to look pink, and darkening the complexion. Thus, a person who had been looking extremely ill before he or she died, with gaunt features and pallid skin,

> BLOOD MIGHT ALSO SEEP FROM THE MOUTH AND NOSE, AS THOUGH IT HAD BEEN FEEDING OFF BLOOD

might possibly, after being buried and exhumed, appear plump and healthy, with rosy cheeks and a ruddy complexion. Blood might also seep from the mouth and nose (as a result of the pressure from the gases), making the corpse look as though it had been feeding off blood. All these signs would be interpreted as evidence of the fact that the individual had, after death, turned into a vampire.

If it was decided that the body must have a stake run through it, to kill the vampire, there might be more signs that would confirm its status in the eye of the ignorant onlooker. Sometimes, a groan would escape from the body, causing onlookers to think that it was alive, and was now in its final death throes. The truth of the matter was that, as the body was pierced, the gases would escape, causing a noise as they passed by the vocal folds, much as gas comes out of the body with a noise when a person breaks wind. There might also be corpses whose hair, nails, and teeth appeared to have grown longer while buried. This, again, had a rational explanation. As skin begins to decompose, it often falls off, leaving more hair, teeth, and nails exposed, and what looks like fresh skin beneath – but, of course, this is only visible because the main part of the skin has died.

Buried alive?

Some commentators have suggested that the myth of the vampire arose in part from the fact that, in certain cases, bodies were buried alive. In an age where people died and were buried without certificates from a doctor, and often without any medical intervention at all, it sometimes happened that a person would show signs of being dead and so be buried, only to revive once underground. In such cases, that person would of course try to raise the alarm, so that sounds of shouting or knocking would be heard emanating from the grave. If this happened, they would perhaps be exhumed, only to be the victim of various gruesome rituals designed to kill off a vampire.

It seems unlikely that this happened very often, if only because it is almost impossible for any human being to survive being buried for any length of time. What appears to be a more credible explanation is that sounds might have been heard coming from a grave, and that these could have been the noise of gas escaping from the cadaver. At this period, with vampire panic at its height, such sounds would have been interpreted as signs of the corpse's life, and thus the body would have been exhumed and dealt with accordingly.

Arnold Paole

A famous vampire case of the eighteenth century was that of Arnold Paole. Paole, also called Paule or Pavle, was a Serbian militiaman who moved to the village of Medveda after living in the part of Serbia controlled at the time by Turkey. He reported having been persecuted by a vampire, and having managed to shake the vampire off by smearing himself with blood from a vampire's grave, and eating the earth around it. In 1726, he died violently in an accident, falling off a haywagon and breaking his neck. About a month after he was buried, several people reported that they were being persecuted by him, and they too died. These deaths were reported to the authorities, who duly investigated, opening up Paole's grave. They found that the body had not decomposed in the normal way, and that there was fresh blood coming out of the corpse's eyes, nose, mouth, and ears. The shroud was also covered in blood. As well as this, his nails appeared to have continued growing. Concluding Paole's

corpse to be a vampire, a stake was driven through his heart, and as this happened, a groan was heard to emanate from the body, further terrifying the villagers. Not only was Paole's corpse disinterred and a stake driven through it, but the alleged victims were also dug up and mutilated in the same way.

These incidents were officially reported and carefully recorded, which is why they are so well documented today. In hindsight, it seems clear that the appearance of Paole's exhumed corpse was nothing to do with the supernatural, but was due entirely to natural causes, and the particular way his body had decomposed.

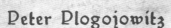

Peter Plogojowitz

Peter Plogojowitz was another renowned vampire case of the period. He was a peasant from a village in a part of Serbia that was under Austrian rule at the time. When Plogojowitz died in 1725, nine other deaths occurred in the area immediately afterwards, within a time span of eight days. All the victims claimed that Plogojowitz had come to their death beds at night and tried to strangle them. There were also rumours that Plogojowitz had visited members of his family, asking them for food and shoes, and that when his son had refused, Plogojowitz had killed him. The villagers demanded that the authorities, in the shape of a man named Frombald, and the local priest, should exhume Plogojowitz's body in case he had turned into a vampire after burial.

When the body was brought out, it seemed to have grown new skin and nails, as well as more hair and a beard. There was 'fresh' blood coming out of its mouth. When the corpse was staked, more apparently fresh blood came out of the ears and mouth. The villagers were extremely frightened, and began to panic, fearing that the vampire could not be killed. Frombald and the priest duly satisfied them that Plogojowitz was indeed dead, and afterwards Frombald filed his report. This became one of the first documented cases about vampires in Eastern Europe, and was widely reported in Germany, England, and France, contributing to the general eighteenth-century panic about vampires.

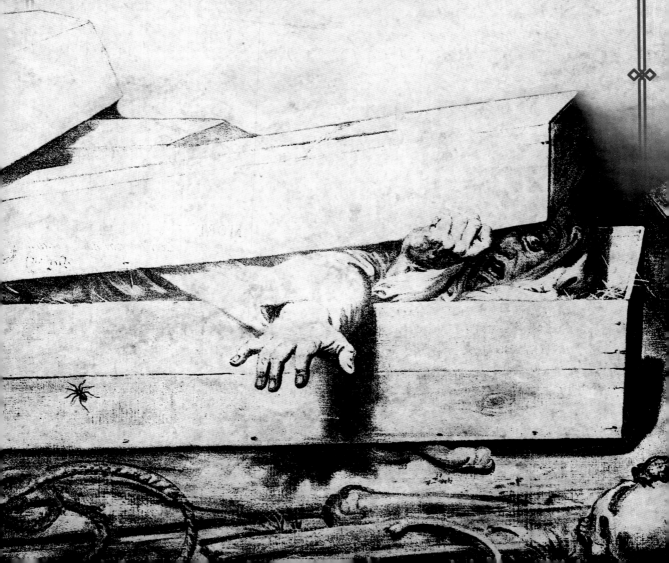

A good-looking corpse

There were numerous other outbreaks of vampire panic in Serbia in the years that followed. In 1731, an official named Dr Glaser investigated a series of deaths that had been blamed on vampirism. After threats from the villagers, he disinterred several of the dead bodies and found that most of them were not decomposed. Instead, they looked plump and had what looked like fresh blood coming out of their mouths. Glaser reported the details of the case to his superiors and recommended that officials should be sent to 'kill' the vampires, so as to satisfy the villagers' superstitions. A military surgeon, Johann Fluckinger, along with others, duly arrived

FRESH BLOOD COMING OUT OF THEIR MOUTHS

to inspect the bodies further. They found that most of them were 'quite complete and undecayed', that they had new nails growing where the old ones had fallen off, and that their skin was 'red and vivid'. In the case of one deceased woman, the body looked better than it had in life: apparently, she had been rather 'dried up' in appearance before her sojourn in the grave, but now she looked the picture of health.

The surgeons duly diagnosed the exhumed corpses to be in 'the vampiric condition', as they put it, and allowed the village elders and some local gypsies to dispose of them as they thought fit. The gypsies cut the heads off the bodies, burned them, and threw the ashes in the river. Once again, when this official report was published, the story aroused tremendous interest, further fuelling the panic about vampires that was beginning to sweep across Europe from the Balkan states.

Vampires & Disease

In the same way that superstitious, uneducated people in the medieval period misunderstood the way corpses naturally decompose after death and burial, there was widespread ignorance about communicable diseases. When a number of deaths among people closely connected in a single town or village occurred, peasant communities often imagined the deaths to be caused by the visitation of a local vampire, rather than attributing the deaths to outbreaks of disease. The vampire in question was often thought to be a neighbour who had died, been buried in a local churchyard, and who was seeking revenge for his or her sudden death by coming back to life as a vampire. The theory was that the vampire would emerge from the grave at night and come back to the village to prey on former family members and friends, trying to suck their blood and in this way achieve immortality. It is possible that this way of thinking arose from primitive feelings of guilt about the fact that, for no apparent reason, some

individuals had died of the disease, while others had survived.

Although it is understandable that epidemics of terminal disease would terrify most ordinary people, as they do today, explanations of them in terms of vampires, evil spirits, and the like were quite damaging to the communities concerned. In the worst cases, they resulted in the persecution of innocent individuals and families: bodies would be dug up and ritually dismembered, burned, or otherwise mutilated. In a traditional, religious society, this would of course have been deeply disturbing for relatives, who would regard such exhumations as a desecration. Even more disturbing, individuals who were still alive, or suffering illness, might be suspected of being vampires, and would be persecuted or shunned.

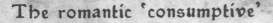

The romantic 'consumptive'

There were a number of diseases that gave rise to specific fears about vampires, mainly connected to the bodily changes they caused. For example, tuberculosis was often thought of as a sign of vampirism. This was related to the fact that sufferers from the disease may cough up blood, and may appear pale. (Significantly, tuberculosis in former times was known as 'consumption', because the sufferer's body appeared to be eaten up from within, echoing the notion of the vampire's bloodsucking ways.) Most commonly, one member of the family would become ill with tuberculosis (TB) and die, while other members became infected and would begin to waste away. As their illness progressed, they would suffer a number of unpleasant traits: their eyes might become red and swollen, and as a result they would develop an aversion to sunlight. Their body temperature would drop, making their skin cold to the touch, like a corpse, and they might become pallid and weak. One traditional story invented to explain this 'wasting away' was that victims had been captured by the fairies and made to dance all night at parties, so that they were exhausted during the day. Another fanciful suggestion was that the sick person had been put under a spell by a witch, transformed into a horse, and forced to carry the witch to her coven at night. Most such tales were an attempt to explain the transformation of a healthy person into a weak, ailing being who might, in some ways, resemble a 'living corpse'.

Later, throughout the eighteenth, nineteenth, and early twentieth centuries, TB remained a widespread terminal disease, and other myths began to surround it: for example, that it was caused by masturbation, or that it produced feelings of feverish euphoria, making artists more creative than they would otherwise have been. Indeed, the Romantics positively fetishized the pallor and waif-like appearance of the 'consumptive', especially in women, emphasizing their fatalistic beauty, as they saw it. This romantic version of the illness soon found its way into vampire lore, with the stories of doomed love that so much appeal to teenagers today.

Porphyria: werewolves and vampires?

Another disease associated with vampirism was porphyria. This is a disease of the blood that is often inherited and whose most unusual symptom is purple discolouration of the faeces and urine (hence the name, which derives from the Greek, meaning, 'purple pigment'). As porphyria is a relatively rare disease, and has many different symptoms, including seizures and hallucinations, it has historically often been attributed to other conditions, including – most irrationally of all – the status of the sufferer as a vampire.

There are several reasons why this explanation should have been put forward. First, porphyria often affects the skin, making it extremely sensitive to light. Necrosis of the skin and gums may occur, so that these parts are eaten away, making teeth and nails look longer. Blisters may erupt on the skin, especially if exposed to the sun. There may be an increase of hair growth in unusual places, such as on the forehead. The sufferer's urine may grow red or purple, and the teeth and fingernails might also appear red. The skin might also appear to glow in the dark. Not surprisingly, in former times, these alarming symptoms were attributed to the supernatural. With their red teeth and nails, and their pale or glowing skins, people with porphyria were often suspected of being vampires. If they grew hair on their faces, they might also be persecuted as werewolves.

In recent years, historians and medical commentators in Britain have advanced the theory that hereditary porphyria affected many of the nobility, including the monarchy. Retrospective diagnoses of the illnesses affecting such monarchs as Mary, Queen of Scots and King George III, have been made, suggesting that they were all suffering from porphyria. This idea has appealed so greatly to novelists, film-makers and the like that it is now commonly assumed to be a matter of fact that there was hereditary porphyria among the British monarchy, and possibly the whole of European nobility. Furthermore, people suppose that this was largely due to intermarriage and inbreeding. In fact, the theory has never been proved and remains a matter of conjecture.

Most of the work done to investigate the link between porphyria and vampirism has resulted in nothing more positive than stigmatizing sufferers from the disease. In 1985, biochemist David Dolphin argued that the age-old connection had arisen since porphyria sufferers in the past might have craved blood. This, he argued, was because consumption of blood eased their symptoms. There was no medical basis to this theory, which seemed to have come

A German woodcut from the fifteenth century of a werewolf attack.

about as a result of misunderstanding the nature of the disease. In addition, Dolphin noted that, in the past, the porphyriac's sensitivity to sunlight could have given rise to the belief that he or she was a vampire. However, as many commentators have pointed out, the idea that vampires are sensitive to sunlight is not originally part of European folklore, but was an addition to the myth introduced in 1922 in the film *Nosferatu*. Despite the weaknesses of Dolphin's medical and cultural research, the theory was widely reported, thus forever establishing the connection between porphyria and vampirism in the public mind.

Rabies: the bite of death

From earliest times, the disease of rabies has terrified human beings. Like TB and porphyria, it transforms the mind and body of the sufferer, but usually more dramatically, in a way that brings agony to the sufferer and horrifies the onlooker. Since rabies is a virus that inflames the brain, it causes acute personality and behavioural changes, and if untreated results in death. And as it is transmitted by animals – humans are usually infected by a bite from an animal such as a dog or a bat – many fears have risen up over the centuries about this phenomenon, and have found their way into folkloric tales of werewolves and vampires.

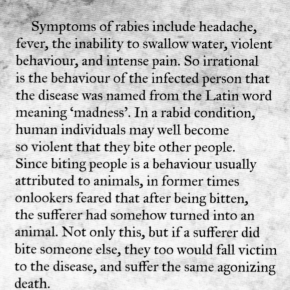

Symptoms of rabies include headache, fever, the inability to swallow water, violent behaviour, and intense pain. So irrational is the behaviour of the infected person that the disease was named from the Latin word meaning 'madness'. In a rabid condition, human individuals may well become so violent that they bite other people. Since biting people is a behaviour usually attributed to animals, in former times onlookers feared that after being bitten, the sufferer had somehow turned into an animal. Not only this, but if a sufferer did bite someone else, they too would fall victim to the disease, and suffer the same agonizing death.

It is easy to see how, in primitive cultures with very little access to scientific knowledge or medical intervention, societies would interpret the phenomenon of rabies as a sign that an evil spirit from an animal source had, through being bitten by a wolf, dog, or bat, entered a human being. For this reason, anxieties about the largely unknown nature and behaviour of nocturnal animals such as bats and wolves, about the bites that these animals may inflict on humans, and about the terrifying consequences of this, have, from time immemorial featured in folklore from across the world. (For more information on this, see Chapter 3). In societies where people lived close to nature, wolves and bats were greatly feared. Wolves were known to attack humans at night; and bats were possibly even more alarming, since they might fly into a house and bite a sleeping individual without them knowing about it. (It is quite possible to be bitten by a bat at night and not to notice the bite the next morning). Thus, folk tales were full of warnings about these rather mysterious animals who could bring such horror to human beings, merely by biting them, and they became part of the mythology of vampires and werewolves.

Vampires & Animals

There are certain animals whose behaviour – for example, hunting at night, and living off human or animal blood and flesh – has always struck fear into human beings. These include bats, wolves, and owls, who play important roles in European folklore, and who also appear, in different guises and with different meanings, in folklore from other parts of the world.

The vampire bat

Of all these, the common vampire bat is perhaps the most ghoulish. The vampire bat lives on a diet of blood, a habit known as haematophagy. As well as the common vampire bat, there are two other kinds of bat that feed solely on blood: the white-winged vampire bat, and the hairy-legged vampire bat. These bloodsucking bats are mostly found in Latin America, and are especially common in Argentina, Chile, and Brazil, where they feature prominently in folk mythology (see Chapter 3).

As we all know, bats hunt at night, and sleep in the day, often in caves. This nocturnal behaviour accords with the vampire legend, in which the vampire only emerges at night, from the cave-like grave, to strike its victims. The body of the vampire bat in particular is well evolved to locate warm-blooded creatures: it has thermoreceptors on its nose, and these help it to find areas on the skin of its victims, such as the neck, where the blood flows close to the surface. It also has relatively large front teeth that it uses to bite into the victim's skin. These teeth have no enamel on them, so they are very sharp. If its victim is an animal whose body is covered in fur, the bat's canine teeth are used to shave off the hair around the area where it makes its incision.

A dinner of blood

The bat's saliva contains a substance called draculin, isolated by Venezuelan researchers working with the common vampire bat in 1995. This functions as an anticoagulant, which stops the blood from the victim clotting, so that the bat can drink it. (This anticoagulant is extremely strong, and thus has been used in medicine to help patients suffering

Engraving of types of cheiroptera. Top is a white boxtailed bat (*Diclidurus albus*) and bottom is a common vampire bat (*Vampyrus spectrum*) from *The Naturalist's Library Mammalia Introduction Vol. VIII*

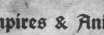
from blood clotting conditions which may result in heart attacks and strokes.) Contrary to what is generally believed, the vampire bat does not suck blood out of the victim's wound, but waits until it begins to pour out, and then laps at it.

Bats have an extremely sensitive hearing system, and the vampire bat is able to detect the sound of sleeping victims, which are their main source of nutrition. The common vampire bat seeks out mammals, while the white-winged vampire bat and the hairy-legged vampire bat feed on birds. Once the vampire bat has found its slumbering prey, it flies over to it and lands silently beside it. Using its infrared sensors, it finds a place to bite, and proceeds to tuck in. Its feed can last as long as 20 minutes, and as it feeds its body quickly digests the blood, and it begins to urinate.

The well-fed bat

After its gruesome dinner, the bat weighs considerably more than it did beforehand. A bat weighing 40 grams can amazingly increase its weight to 60; thus it can eat up to half its weight in blood. So its next problem is how to fly off. It does this by crouching down and hurling itself into the air, propelling itself upwards and flying quickly to its roost, before settling down for a good long sleep. After a few days, the blood fully digested, the bat will be hungry again, and ready to seek out its next victim.

Most animals or humans bitten by a vampire bat in this way, while they are sleeping, will not know what has happened, as the actual bite is small and causes no pain. It is rather similar to being bitten by a mosquito. However, some bats may carry serious diseases such as rabies, so for this reason, it is unwise to handle them, or to allow them into the house. This has been known since ancient times, and bats are avoided as a consequence. The old wives' tale about getting bats tangled in the hair has no real foundation, however, it may have arisen because gnat-eating bats appear to sometimes dart towards the heads of human beings at dusk.

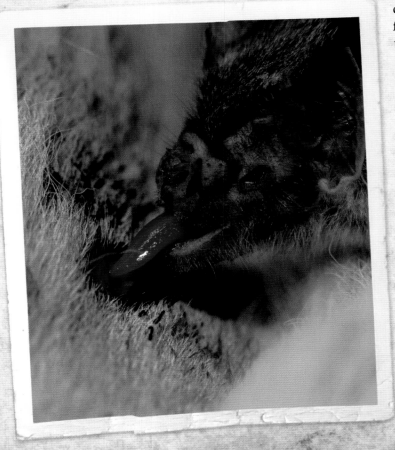

A vampire bat drinks blood from a sleeping calf

Howling wolf

For centuries, in many parts of the world, human beings have lived side by side with wolves. Not surprisingly, these enigmatic creatures figure heavily in the folklore and mythology of these regions. In some cultures, notably Native American and Nordic, they are regarded with awe and respect. However, in Slavic folklore, they tend to be seen in a negative light, in stories that emphasize their hunting as bloodthirsty and aggressive, and their twilight howling, which can be heard for miles, as eerie and threatening. There are also many European tales of werewolves, in which human beings transform into hybrid creatures capable of great violence and destruction. Some of these stories originate partly in the observed behaviour of the wolf, while others are in the realm of pure fantasy.

The European grey wolf is generally thought to be the wild ancestor of the domesticated dog. It has survived since earliest times as a predator, though today its numbers are depleted, and as a rule it no longer lives side by side with human beings (except in a few countries, such as Romania). Wolves can run fast, up to 40 miles an hour, and have great stamina. Their relatively large feet, with a slight webbing between the toes, help them to navigate difficult terrains, including snow, and their thick winter coats insulate them from water as well as cold. They have yellow eyes, long legs, and strong teeth for holding their prey, crushing its bones, and tearing off its flesh. They are known to be carriers of many killer diseases, including rabies and anthrax. If suffering from rabies, they can become extremely aggressive, and can run wild, biting and killing many people.

RIGHT: Werewolves, illustration for *Legendes Rustiques* by George Sand, 1858

Children as prey

Wolves have a strong pack mentality, with a hierarchical system of dominant and submissive members, and mark out their territory by a system of communication that includes scent marking (with urine, faeces, and pheromones from their scent glands) and howling. At twilight, many members of the pack may gather together and howl, which is a way of communicating that their territory is out of bounds to other packs. They hunt mainly hooved or pawed animals, but also subsist on carcasses killed by other animals, and rubbish left outside by humans. When they catch their prey, they first tear at the legs, to stop it running away; then they may sever the windpipe,

biting at the head and neck. If catching prey smaller than themselves, they will grab the animal, carry them off, and feed on them in a private place. This may happen while the prey is still alive. When the wolves begin to eat an animal, such as a deer, they will begin with the liver, lungs, and heart. They will continue with the stomach, the leg muscles, and finally, the hide and the bones, until almost nothing is left.

Before the twentieth century, wolf attacks on humans were a well-known though not very common occurrence. However, the damage to livestock was extensive, and this is perhaps why wolves came to be hated in many parts of Europe. There were also incidences of small children being carried off by wolves, and this may have led to fairy tales that warned children of this danger. It may also have inspired mythological stories of children being raised in the wild by a wolf pack.

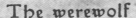
The werewolf

Fear of wolves also gave rise to stories of werewolves, which along with vampires, dominated European folk tales in the medieval period. The werewolf is a legendary creature, a human being who has the ability to shift its shape into a wolf or wolf-like animal with tremendous strength and supernatural powers. The transformation occurs under a full moon, and is accompanied by much howling and gnashing of teeth as the body painfully changes shape, growing fangs, fur, and yellow eyes. The first writer to record such a creature is the medieval commentator, Gervase of Tilbury, but similar creatures appear in the writings of the Ancient Greeks, notably Petronius.

> **THE TRANSFORMATION OCCURS UNDER A FULL MOON, AND IS ACCOMPANIED BY MUCH HOWLING AND GNASHING OF TEETH**

It has been argued that, as with the vampire legends, the tales of werewolves may have arisen to explain the occurrence of diseases such as rabies and porphyria. If bitten by a rabid wolf, an infected human being might take on the aggressive behaviour of an angry wolf or dog. In the case of porphyria, bloodshot eyes and reddened teeth, as well as sensitivity to light, might mark a sufferer out as a werewolf. However, there is some controversy about these suggestions, in that the classic werewolf tales do not necessarily involve reference to transmission of the condition through biting. (This is in contrast to the vampire legend, which definitely does entail the idea of people becoming vampires as a result of being bitten.) In both the case of the vampire and the werewolf, the issue of light sensitivity, which is a characteristic of porphyria, seems to be irrelevant, since this was not mentioned in either case in early folklore tales.

It seems more likely that the werewolf in European folklore is a symbol that helps to explain many strange human behaviours, for example, mental illnesses in which individuals appear to have a dual personality – gentle one minute, violent the next. Or it may simply be a way of describing how the world becomes more frightening and strange at night, especially in remote rural areas, when the wolves begin to howl and human beings are reminded of how precarious their civilization is, and how easily it might be destroyed. The anthropologist Robert Eisler touched on the psychological connection between humans and wolves in his study *Man into Wolf*, reflecting that when early tribes changed from being hunter gatherers to predatory hunters, they began to identify with the predatory wolf. (This may also help to explain the preponderance of wolf-derived Christian and surnames in Northern Europe, such as the German male Christian names Adalwolf, and Wolfgang meaning noble wolf and wolf path, and the Spanish surname, Lopez, which means simply – wolf.)

The vampire werewolf

Inevitably, the werewolf legend soon became tangled, in medieval folklore, with that of the vampire. In Europe, people suspected of being werewolves were often executed, and their bodies burned rather than being buried. This was because there was a widespread belief that werewolves might, after death, turn into vampires. These vampires might come back to life as hyenas – another creature with a long history of negative associations in human culture. As a scavenger feeding off dead or dying animals, including humans, the hyena is reviled in most societies (indeed the word 'hyena' in Greek derives from 'pig'), and in the past has been thought of as the companion of demons and witches. Traditionally, hyenas are regarded as hybrid creatures whose sexuality is indeterminate, and they are much feared throughout the world, particularly in Africa, where night attacks on humans have occurred, in some instances, proving fatal. The curious laughing call of the Spotted Hyena (which actually hunts live prey) has also been the source of much dislike of the animal.

Not only werewolves, but sinners, were thought to come back to life after they had died. In addition, people with pale faces, hollow eyes, and swollen lips, were suspected of being werewolves, and persecuted as a result. It was feared that when they died, either of natural causes or because they were executed, they would take the form of blood-drinking wolves, coming back to the corpse they had left behind at break of day. In order to avoid this, priests would be sent to perform exorcisms. Disinterring and decapitating the dead body, and often throwing the head into a river, where it was hoped it would sink, due to the weight of the many sins within it.

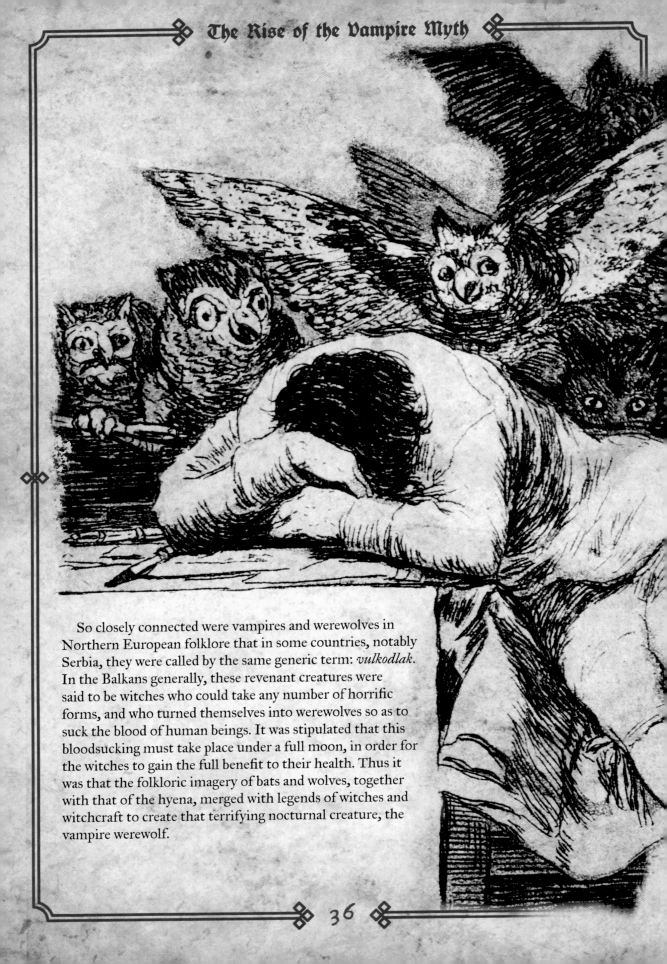

So closely connected were vampires and werewolves in Northern European folklore that in some countries, notably Serbia, they were called by the same generic term: *vulkodlak*. In the Balkans generally, these revenant creatures were said to be witches who could take any number of horrific forms, and who turned themselves into werewolves so as to suck the blood of human beings. It was stipulated that this bloodsucking must take place under a full moon, in order for the witches to gain the full benefit to their health. Thus it was that the folkloric imagery of bats and wolves, together with that of the hyena, merged with legends of witches and witchcraft to create that terrifying nocturnal creature, the vampire werewolf.

The owl of doom

Along with the bat and the wolf, the other creature to be associated with vampirism – and, of course, with witches – is the owl. As everybody knows, owls usually hunt at twilight or during the night, and mostly prey on small mammals. They have extraordinary powers of vision, and their feathers are constructed in such a way that they make little sound as they fly along. The feathers may also be delicately marked so as to camouflage them from their victim. Owls use their sharp talons and beak to catch their prey and often swallow it whole, later regurgitating indigestible parts of it, such as bones and fur, in small pellets.

The familiar hoot or screech of the owl as it hunts has long been associated, in human culture, with death and destruction. The ancient Strix of Roman mythology (see Chapter 3) is based on the owl, and in Romania, the call of the owl is traditionally thought to presage the death of someone nearby. However, the owl is also thought to be wise (for instance, as the companion of Minerva, the Ancient Greek goddess of wisdom). Thus, like the wolf, the owl has positive as well as negative associations in human culture.

Rules and taboos

In conclusion, we can see how the habits of bats, wolves, and owls have contributed to the vampire legend, both in Europe and around the rest of the world. Historically, humans have lived close to these animals, and have come to fear them, in some cases quite rationally, in other cases rather foolishly. Folk tales and legends of vampirism express these fears, and may also set rules and taboos – some sensible, some wildly irrational – about how to minimize their perceived threat to human life.

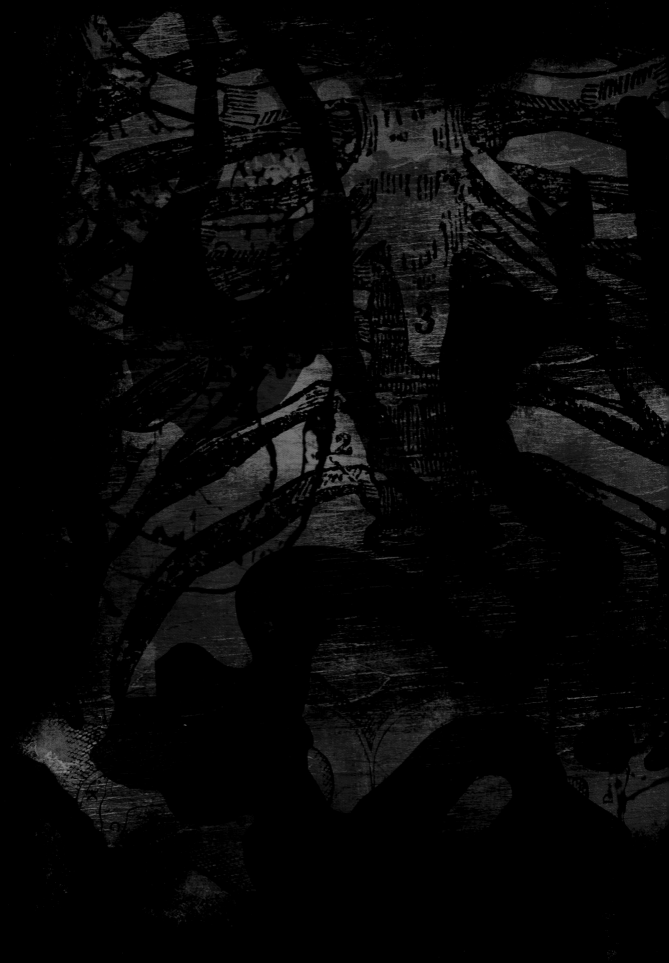

CHAPTER 2

From Peasant to Nobleman

In contrast to the vampires described in popular literature of the nineteenth century, the medieval vampire did not have fangs; it was not pale or gaunt; it had no aversion to sunlight; nor did it have any sophistication or charisma. It certainly did not appear to its victims dressed immaculately for an upper-class dinner or ball, or sporting a long red cape. The whole sexual element, of a charming, smooth-talking, upper-class individual, was entirely missing in medieval stories. These characteristics were later additions to the myth, that came about as the vampire myth began to find its way into popular literature once the eighteenth-century panic about vampire sightings had died down.

'An enormous corpulence'

As far as we know from writings of the time, the medieval vampire was conceived of as a repellent creature with no sexual allure whatsoever. On the contrary, it was foul-smelling and ugly, and people would flee as soon as it appeared. There are several reports about sightings of vampires that date from this early period. One of the most graphic is that of William of Newburgh, also known as William Parvus, a twelfth-century English historian who made a study of 'revenants', that is, the deceased who come back from the dead.

In one case, Newburgh described a man of 'evil conduct', who escaped from jail and died when he fell out of the rafters of the roof in his bedroom (where he was hiding to spy on his wife, who was having an affair.) Newburgh relates that the man had a Christian burial, but that he later arose from his grave and wandered around the town, pursued by a pack of barking dogs. He killed a number of townspeople, terrorizing them into staying at home with their doors locked as soon as the sun went down. Eventually, the local people tired of this, and decided to trap the vampire in his lair. They went to the graveyard, dug up the man's corpse, and laid it bare. A horrible sight awaited them. The corpse, as Newburgh describes it, was 'swollen to an enormous corpulence, with its countenance beyond measure turgid and suffused with blood; while the napkin in which it had been wrapped appeared nearly torn to pieces.' He continues: 'The young men, however, spurred on by wrath, feared not, and inflicted a wound upon the senseless carcass, out of which incontinently flowed such a stream of blood,

that it might have been taken for a leech filled with the blood of many persons. Then, dragging it beyond the village, they speedily constructed a funeral pile; and upon one of them saying that the pestilential body would not burn unless its heart were torn out, the other laid open its side by repeated blows of the blunted spade, and, thrusting in his hand, dragged out the accursed heart.'

More fat vampires

By the eighteenth century, belief in vampires had reached a peak, so much so that a number of studies into the phenomenon were published, many of them by respected scholars. The most famous of these was by Augustin Calmet, a Benedictine scholar from Lorraine in France. In 1746, he presented his treatise, *Dissertation on the apparition of angels, demons, and spirits; and on revenants and vampires in Hungary, Bohemia, Moravia, and Silesia.* Calmet wrongly supposed that the idea of the vampire as a reanimated corpse who survived by sucking blood was a new one, dating the phenomenon to the late seventeenth century. He wrote: 'In this age, a new scene presents itself to our eyes and has done for about sixty years. In Hungary, Moravia, Silesia and Poland, men, it is said, who have been dead for several months, come back to earth, talk, walk, infest villages, ill use both men and beasts, suck the blood of their near relations, destroy their health and finally cause their death; so that people can only save themselves from their dangerous visits and their hauntings, by exhuming them, impaling them, cutting off their heads, tearing out their hearts, or burning them. These are called by the name of oupires or vampires, that is to say, leeches ... In the twelfth century also, in England and Denmark, some resuscitations similar to those of Hungary were seen. But in no history do we read anything similar, so common, or so decided, as what is related to us of the vampires of Poland, Hungary and Moravia.'

In his treatise, Calmet carefully presented a collection of descriptions and sightings of vampires, but he himself remained ambivalent about their existence. Many of those who read his essay, however, took it to be positive proof that vampires were, indeed, stalking the land, and overall, it supported the superstitions about revenants. However, another Frenchman, Francois-Marie Arouet, better known by his pen name Voltaire, was extremely sceptical about

Calmet's findings, and in his *Philosophical Dictionary*, published in 1764, he employed his sharp wit to poke fun at the idea:

These vampires were corpses, who went out of their graves at night to suck the blood of the living, either at their throats or stomachs, after which they returned to their cemeteries. The persons so sucked waned, grew pale, and fell into consumption; while the sucking corpses grew fat, got rosy, and enjoyed an excellent appetite. It was in Poland, Hungary, Silesia, Moravia, Austria, and Lorraine, that the dead made this good cheer.

Bela Lugosi (1882-1956) in the 1931 production of *Dracula* in threatening pose with young lady

'A barbarism of ignorance'

Despite Voltaire's mocking review, Calmet's treatise had such influence that the Empress Maria of Austria finally sent her personal physician, Gerard van Swieten, to investigate the claims of vampirism in her territories. Like Voltaire, van Swieten was sceptical about the existence of vampires, but nonetheless he wrote a serious report about the allegations, entitled, *A Discourse on the Existence of Ghosts*. In this essay, published in 1768, he explained how the body decomposed, and how blood and gases might account for the ruddy complexion and swollen appearance of recently buried corpses. In conclusion he called the vampire myth 'a barbarism of ignorance', and said, '...all the fuss is nothing but a vain fear, a superstitious credulity, a dark and eventful imagination, simplicity and ignorance among the people.' As a result of van Swieten's findings, the Empress issued an edict forbidding people to exhume, mutilate, and burn buried corpses.

The aristocratic vampire

After this, the exhumations of corpses and persecution of living people with abnormalities of any kind thankfully died down. However, stories of vampires continued to thrill audiences, and were taken up in popular literature of all kinds. In the early nineteenth century, a suave and sophisticated vampire made its first appearance in John Polidori's *The Vampyre*, published in 1819. (For more information on this, and other literary vampires, see Chapter 5). In appearance, Polidori's vampire was a complete contrast to his forebears; instead of being 'fat and rosy', he was pale, thin, and good-looking. Polidori describes him thus: 'It happened that in the midst of the dissipations attendant upon a London winter, there appeared at the various parties of

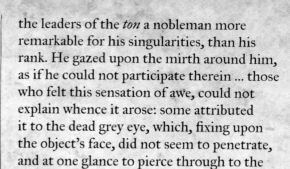

the leaders of the *ton* a nobleman more remarkable for his singularities, than his rank. He gazed upon the mirth around him, as if he could not participate therein ... those who felt this sensation of awe, could not explain whence it arose: some attributed it to the dead grey eye, which, fixing upon the object's face, did not seem to penetrate, and at one glance to pierce through to the inward workings of the heart ...'

Despite, or perhaps because of his deathly, soul-searching gaze, this intriguing stranger was extremely attractive to the female sex:

A 'winning tongue'

'His peculiarities caused him to be invited to every house; all wished to see him, and those who had been accustomed to violent excitement, and now felt the weight of ennui, were pleased at having something in their presence capable of engaging their attention. In spite of the deadly hue of his face, which never gained a warmer tint, either from the blush of modesty, or from the strong emotion of passion, though its form and outline were beautiful, many of the female hunters after notoriety attempted to win his attentions, and gain, at least, some marks of what they might term affection.'

Polidori's vampire was not only physically alluring, he also had a 'winning tongue', and his 'apparent hatred of vice' – he routinely ignored all the women who threw themselves at him – made him even more fascinating.

In creating his aristocratic vampire, Polidori set a template for virtually all the vampire figures that followed. Bram Stoker, author of the seminal *Dracula*, which was published in 1897, drew heavily on his idea of the vampire as a charming, intelligent, refined, and sophisticated man about town, and this incarnation of the vampire went on to become a staple of the horror genre up to the present day.

Baby Vampires

In the Middle Ages, the timing of a baby's birth had much significance – negative as well as positive. In the same way, details of its appearance could have all kinds of mysterious meanings. Its lineage was also a matter of great importance: for example, the seventh son of the seventh son might be considered to have supernatural powers, or other extraordinary features. As the vampire myth spread from the Balkans and took hold of the popular imagination in Europe, these superstitions about the circumstances of a baby's birth became entwined with the vampire myth, so that when a new baby came into the world, it would be checked for tell-tale signs, and possibly rejected as a result.

The caul: blessing or curse?

First and foremost were birth defects and abnormalities, some of which would be considered normal enough today. For example, if the baby was born in a caul, it would be viewed as suspicious. A caul is a membrane from the amniotic sac which separates the baby from the wall of its mother's womb. At birth, instead of leaving this caul behind, the baby occasionally emerges wrapped inside it. Today, a doctor or midwife usually breaks this membrane during the mother's labour, if it does not rupture of its own accord during the process; thus babies born in the caul are less common now than they used to be.

In health terms, being born in a caul poses no risks, and is positively beneficial to the baby, in that it is shielded from infection until the caul peels off spontaneously. In medieval peasant societies with little access to medical help, it was noted that babies born in the caul were often stronger and healthier than most, and had a better chance of survival. A membrane strong enough to withstand the process of labour was seen as protective. For this reason, the caul was seen as a sign of good luck, and could signify that the child would be a successful individual in later life. In many cases, the caul would be kept as an heirloom: the midwife would rub some paper on the baby's head, so that the membrane would transfer onto the paper, and then present it to the mother.

The caul was also thought to have special powers, for example to protect against black magic, to defend the harvest, and to ensure fertility. Cauls were also thought to protect the bearer from drowning: in medieval times, women would sell cauls to sailors for this reason. There was also a belief that a caulbearer could prophesy the future, especially through dreams. Twins born with a caul would be believed to be protected by a guardian angel throughout life. In Iceland, the baby born with a caul was said to have a fairy companion, known as a 'fylgiar', who would serve it throughout life, even foretelling its death and travelling with it to Valhallah, the home of the dead.

All this changed, however, when the vampire myth came to be popularized. If a baby was born with a caul, it was feared that it might become a vampire. The caul would be removed immediately in case the baby tried to eat it, which was highly unlikely, and instead of being kept as a valuable talisman, the caul would be destroyed as quickly as possible.

IF A BABY WAS BORN WITH A CAUL, IT WAS FEARED THAT IT MIGHT BECOME A VAMPIRE

Still from the Larry Cohen movie, *It's Alive*.

Babies with teeth

Another disturbing sign of possible vampirism was a baby born with teeth. In most cases, babies are born with the tooth buds, as they are called, inside the gums. However, in some cases (about one in every 2,000), babies are born with what are called 'natal teeth'. These are the infant's primary teeth that have come through the gums early. It is extremely rare for a baby to have a full set of these teeth, but up to seven or eight teeth have been observed. In most instances, the natal teeth pose no real problems, although they may be removed if they are loose, to prevent the baby swallowing one and choking on it. The teeth may also cause feeding problems, as the baby may bite the mother's nipple. Today, it is generally considered best to leave the teeth to grow naturally, as early removal can lead to difficulties later on, when all the teeth push through the gums.

It is not difficult to see why a baby born with such teeth might be feared as a vampire. In many cases, only the two incisors at either side of the top gum are present, giving the baby the distinct appearance of a small vampire. When the baby started to feed, and accidentally bit the mother's nipple, this would have been seen as further evidence that a vampire child had been born.

The extra nipple

Any kind of birth defect or abnormality would also, in medieval times, be taken as a sign that the child might be a vampire: for example, a third nipple, which occurs in about one in 18 people (though many of these extra nipples look like moles, and are never noticed). The nipple is usually found along either of two 'milk lines' on the stomach, running from under the armpit, through the nipples on the chest, and down into the groin. These 'milk lines' mimic the arrangement of nipples on the underbelly of female animals such as wolves. They may vary in degree from a simple patch of hair to a miniature milk-bearing mammary gland. In some cases, nipples appear on the arms, on the legs, and even, very rarely, on the feet.

Once again, one can imagine why such extra nipples might be taken as a sign that a newborn might not be fully human, but could be a witch, a vampire, or a werewolf. There are instances of this belief in history. For example, Anne Boleyn, the second wife of the English monarch Henry VIII, was rumoured to have a third nipple. There were even stories that she had a third breast, which is another known, but rarer, condition. However, we do not know whether this story is true, since in those days, such abnormalities were considered to be the mark of a witch, and since Anne Boleyn was such a controversial figure (King Henry had divorced his first wife to marry her), these rumours may well have been entirely without basis.

Hair and birthmarks

Other traits in babies were also considered to be signs that they were or might become vampires. In Slavic folklore, children born with red hair and blue eyes were suspect, as were babies born with a lot of hair on their bodies. Birthmarks were also thought of as unlucky and a possible sign of future depravity. Sadly, such babies might be rejected by their mothers, or if not, the nursing pair might be shunned by the rest of the community. This is one of the more negative aspects of the vampire cult, in that it was used to persecute individuals and families who suffered from physical

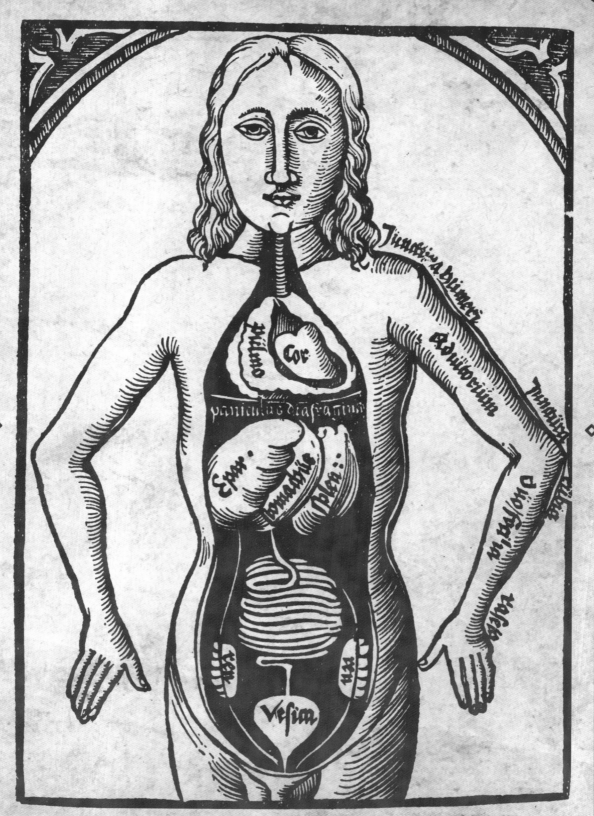

Circa 1500, Anatomical drawing showing heart and intestines by Jodocus Truttvetler von Eisenach

abnormalities, or who looked unusual in any way. Thus, traits that might at one time have been seen as distinctive, conferring high status, took on a darker significance as signs that an evil vampire had come into the world.

Warding off evil

In order to ward off evil, peasant families would employ a number of superstitious rituals. For example, when a family member died, the clocks in the house would be stopped, and mirrors covered. There was a strong belief that the spirit of a corpse could become trapped in a mirror, or that if a living person was reflected in a mirror with the corpse, they would die soon after. Underlying this taboo was the idea that the image of a person in a mirror is the image of their soul. (When vampires look in the mirror, there is no reflection, because they have lost their souls.) Mourners would also be warned not to let their shadows fall over the corpse, because this, too, might have the unfortunate effect of sparking an evil spirit into life.

In addition, families used many 'apotropaics' (items designed to turn away evil spirits). Holy water would be sprinkled over the threshold of the house, and strings of garlic hung up around the kitchen. The crucifix and rosary were considered to be powerful deterrents to vampires. Wild roses were also thought to have magical properties that could help to ward off evil spirits.

In the graveyard, poppy seeds were often sprinkled around the grave after a burial. Legend had it that when a vampire woke up and decided go on the prowl, it would first have to pick up all the poppy seeds around the grave, so this was a way of slowing down its progress. It was also believed that if a body was buried at a crossroads instead of a graveyard, this might confuse the vampire,

who would head off in the wrong direction should it decide to go looking for victims.

Other rather obscure beliefs were commonly held, such as the idea that pregnant women should eat salt so as to prevent giving birth to a vampire. Burying a body with a piece of iron in its hand, or placing a sprig of hawthorn in the coffin, were also trusted remedies for vampirism.

As people went about their daily routines, they would be careful to observe certain practices designed to keep vampires away. Children might be warned to take a long route home rather than pass a graveyard where vampires might lurk. In some cases, if people had to travel into areas that might be haunted by vampires, they would disguise themselves so that the vampire would not recognize them.

⊹❖ Vampire Detection ❖⊹

As the vampire myth developed, more and more signs of vampirism found their way into popular culture. Ancient superstitions were remembered, and became part of the vampire cult, beginning with the timing of the baby's birth.

According to Southern Slavic folklore, a child born between Christmas and Epiphany had a high chance of becoming a vampire. In Romania, the seventh child in a family was also suspect, especially if his or her older siblings were all the same sex. Moreover, illegitimate babies, and premature babies, even those born in wedlock, were regarded with suspicion as potential vampires.

Once born, the child continued to be under intense scrutiny for signs of evil intent. If a baby was weaned early, or was suckled after it had already been weaned, it could suddenly turn into a vampire. And a baby who died before being baptized was almost certain to become a vampire and haunt the family after it was buried.

Vampire signs

If the child survived into adulthood — and many did not — its path continued to be fraught with danger. A person who happened to eat the remains of a sheep killed by a wolf, either by accident or on purpose, could turn into a vampire; thus

The end of a Bohemian vampire – his coffin is opened, and a red-hot iron is plunged into his evil heart.

'wolf kill' was generally avoided by villagers and townspeople alike. It was also believed that a person who had been attacked seven times without dying must have supernatural powers, and therefore was a vampire. If a person sustained an open wound, it had to be treated with boiling water immediately, otherwise this could lead to becoming a vampire. Being excommunicated from the established church could also be a trigger to vampirism, since people who rebelled against religion were greatly feared. And a pregnant woman who was attacked by a vampire would be bound to give birth to a vampire baby.

> ## IF THE STAKE WAS MADE OF ROSEWOOD OR ASH, IT WAS CONSIDERED TO BE DOUBLY EFFECTIVE

The superstitions did not end there. People who had small and insignificant physical abnormalities, such as sharp, pointed tongues and long incisors, were routinely classed as vampires, and at best, given a wide berth; at worst, they were mercilessly persecuted, and in some cases, even killed. Low-life members of society such as prostitutes, alcoholics, murderers and rapists were also shunned, not only for the way they had decided to live their lives, but also because it was believed that they would become vampires after they had been buried. This was also true of people that committed suicide or had died a violent death. Not surprisingly, the offspring of a supposed witch and a werewolf was also to be avoided, since he or she would almost certainly be a vampire.

Eternal damnation

If living people were a target for superstitions about vampirism, the dead were even more so. Once a person died, it seemed that the vampire myth went into overdrive.

As mentioned, the Slavic 'old religion' was full of beliefs about the spirits of the dead, who were considered to thrive, side by side, with the living, watching to see how their former families, friends, and neighbours behaved now that they had gone. Underlying these beliefs was a sense that the dead were jealous of the living, and might take their revenge in any way. The Christian church's teaching on immortality was twisted so that, instead of life after death being a reward for having lived a decent, honest life, it became a form of eternal damnation, with the vampire emerging from its lonely grave to wreak its evil revenge on the living.

Horrific mutilations

For this reason, a number of quite horrific mutilations were performed on the dead body before it was buried. As we all know, piercing the heart of the body with a wooden stake was thought to kill a vampire, preventing it from rising up from the grave and stalking its prey at night. If the stake was made of rosewood or ash, it was considered to be doubly effective.

But there were many other 'precautions' taken, too. For example, the head might be cut off, and the feet, so as to stop the vampire from walking into the village from the churchyard. The head would then be buried under the buttocks, so that it would not be able to get out from underneath the body when it came to life. In other cases, the heart might be taken out and put on top of the head. Bodies were often mutilated, and the body parts tied together in a bundle before being placed in the grave. Occasionally, nails would be driven into the head.

Virgins and stallions

Other, slightly less gruesome, but equally superstitious 'precautions' were taken to prevent dead bodies from becoming vampires. The eyes might be weighted down with coins, to prevent the vampire from seeing when it woke up. The mouth might be tied closed, so that it could not go on to bite its victims, or stuffed with garlic, which was considered a powerful apotropaic, or deterrent (for more information on this, see page 57). There is a parallel with this among the Ancient Greeks, who used to place a silver coin in the deceased's mouth. In the past, historians believed this was done so that the dead person could pay the toll to the ferryman on the River Styx and pass through to the underworld, but more recently, it has been interpreted as a means of preventing evil spirits entering the body. This would accord with the Greek folkloric figure of the 'vrykolas', a harmful undead creature very similar, and possibly related to, the Slavic vampire.

Sometimes, a thorn might be placed under the dead body's tongue. The corpse might be buried with a sickle around its neck, or a needle inserted into the navel. It was also common practice to break the legs of the corpse and to cut the knee ligaments. Further precautions included burying the corpse face down, or burning it to ashes, and then scattering the ashes over a nearby river.

Once the body was safely in the grave, the anxiety still did not cease. Any number of elaborate rituals were performed to keep it there, and to determine whether or not the burial rites had succeeded in stopping the body from transforming into a vampire. One rather bizarre method was to lead a virgin boy sitting on a virgin stallion through the churchyard. In Albania, the stallion in question had to be black, while in other countries it had to be white. If a vampire was lurking in one of the graves, the stallion would refuse to walk past

it. Needless to say, this method did not prove foolproof, and often bodies would be disinterred only to find that they were peacefully rotting away with no sign of vampirism upon them.

Again, connected to the Slavic 'old religion' was the belief that the corpse must be carefully guarded in case it suddenly came alive after death. Until it was buried, a corpse could never be left alone. The guardian also had to keep a sharp eye out for dogs and cats, because if one jumped over the corpse, it might become a vampire. This is a superstition that, strangely enough, occurs in China as well as the Slavic countries.

Vampire exorcism

Much of what we know today about medieval superstitions concerning vampires comes from archaeologists, who have found remains of mutilated skeletons buried for hundreds of years. For example, in 2009, the body of a woman was unearthed from a mass grave on the Venetian island of Lazzaretto Nouvo, Italy. Her skull had a large brick shoved into its mouth, leading archaeologists to believe that she had been suspected of being a vampire. The brick was there to weigh her down and prevent her from leaving the grave. It was particularly important that she remained where she was because, along with the others in the grave, she was a victim of the bubonic plague that swept through Venice in 1576, killing up to 50,000 people.

The archaeologists thought that the corpse of the woman had been seen by gravediggers, who noticed that she had decomposed in an alarming way, and therefore decided to put the brick into her skull. At that time, it was uncommon for a grave to be opened soon after burial; graves were only opened after hundreds of years, by which time all that would have remained of the body was the skeleton, or parts of it. Thus, most ordinary people did not know what a recently decomposing body looked like. The gravediggers, who during the plague, had to frequently open the graves to add further corpses, may have mistaken the 'purge fluid' of the woman's body – that is, a dark fluid from the gastrointestinal tract that can flow out of the nose and mouth after death – for fresh blood, and assumed that she had been eating live flesh.

Not only this, but there was a hole in the shroud around the skeleton's mouth, which made it look as though she had been biting through it in an effort to escape. The archaeologists argued that the woman's bodily fluids would have wet the

shroud, causing it to sink into the cavity of the mouth and dissolve there. Putting the stone into the corpse's mouth, it seems, was an act of exorcism designed to stop her rising from the grave and spreading her disease.

Interestingly, the archaeologists in this case also argued that, during times of plague, vampire legends spread more widely. This was because tombs, sepulchres, and mass graves were opened so frequently, gravediggers had the opportunity to see recently decomposing bodies, which normally did not happen – and it was also a good answer to why people were dying at such a rapid rate. Naturally enough, the discovery of the so-called 'vampire corpses' only spread further alarm at such times of pestilence.

Remains of a female 'vampire' from sixteenth-century Venice, buried with a brick in her mouth to prevent her from rising from her grave and feasting on the living. She was most probably a victim of the bubonic plague that swept through Venice in 1576.

❖ Vampire 'Lifestyles' ❖

Just as the myths about vampires' appearance and character developed through the centuries, so too did stories about their behaviour. The habits attributed to them differed according to the region or country where the variant of the legend arose.

In Bavaria, for example, vampires were said to sleep in their coffins with their thumbs crossed and one eye open. In other European countries, vampires were thought to stalk the streets wearing their shrouds, or the clothes they had been buried in. In Moravia, vampires were alleged to be naked when they made their attacks. Albanian vampires were always described as wearing high-heeled shoes, and legend had it that inside the heels of their shoes, they carried the soil of their native land.

Vampires were essentially undead spirits, and like other poltergeists, they might misbehave from time to time; throwing stones at roofs or windows, breaking or moving household objects, and pulling people's legs or arms as they slept. There were also stories that they pressed on sleeping individuals, perhaps trying to suffocate them. In some cultures, it was believed that a vampire could not enter a house unless it was invited in by the householder. However, once the vampire was let in, it might come and go as it pleased. For this reason, it was thought dangerous to let strangers into the house.

———❧———

The plague bringer

A widely held belief about vampires was that they brought plagues to cattle, sheep, and other livestock. When a communicable disease broke out in a community, it was often attributed to vampires. The fact that these mythical creatures came to life at night, and that people were often too frightened to go out and find out what they were doing, contributed to all sorts of fearful fantasies about what they got up to on their nightly wanderings. Thus the vampire myth gained credibility, and as late as the nineteenth century, communities in New England still believed vampires to be responsible for outbreaks of tuberculosis. In 1892 in Rhode Island, a 19-year-old girl called Mercy Brown, died and was buried. Two months later, suspected of being a vampire, she was dug up by her father, and the family doctor cut out her heart, and burned her to ashes.

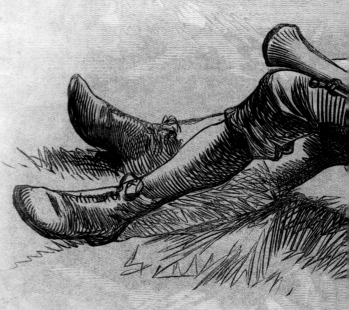

Fear of sunlight

Although the vampire was said to rise from the grave at night and return there in the morning, in early folklore there was no suggestion that it might be vulnerable to sunlight. Even in nineteenth century vampire literature, there was little mention of the notion that sunlight could kill a vampire. On the contrary, vampires were thought to move around like ordinary people during the daytime, their supernatural powers only coming upon them at night.

The idea that sunlight was harmful to vampires was an addition to the mythology that took place in the twentieth century, and went on to appear in comics, books, films, and on television. In these later stories, vampires might collapse or explode when hit by sunlight, the 'scientific' explanation for this being that their neural pathways would fire randomly in their brains, causing them to experience extreme epileptic reactions, blinding them, and possibly setting them on fire. Obviously, this idea was appealing to film-makers and comic strip artists, but it had no real basis in the traditional mythology of vampirism.

Fear of water and fire

Vampires were also said to be terrified of water. In some cultures, they were thought to be unable to cross over any stretch of water, such as walking over the river on a bridge, and for this reason, churchyards were often sited by ponds and rivers. Throwing water over a vampire, especially holy water that had been blessed by a priest, was believed, among Slavic communities, to have the power to destroy it, and this aspect of vampire mythology has continued through the centuries to the present day.

The vampire's fear of water has an interesting connection to hydrophobia, a sympton of rabies, in which sufferers experience intense terror of water as part of their madness. The explanation behind this connection may be that, in the past, people suffering from rabies as a result of being bitten by a bat or wolf exhibited insane behaviour, including fear of water, in the last stages of the disease, and for this reason they may have been deemed to have turned into

Still from *Let the Right One In*, where Eli has entered a home that she has not been invited into.

a vampire – hence the idea that vampires hate water and may be destroyed by it.

In traditional folklore, fire and sunlight are other sources of fear for vampires. This is seemingly due to their pallid skin tone and love for darkness. Even a flame from a candle was believed to send them into a state of psychotic fear. Therefore it is not surprising that people believed that one of the most effective methods for killing a vampire was to burn their body to ashes. In most cases, the head and heart would be removed before the cremation took place. Traditional folklore stipulated that the body must be burned thoroughly, as vampires had a supernatural ability to heal themselves, and could come to life again if the job was not done properly.

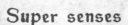

Super senses

Another odd characteristic of the vampire, as it appears in ancient folklore, was that it had a very sensitive sense of smell. For this reason, garlic was said to ward off vampires – they simply could not bear the smell. During church services, garlic would be handed out to ensure that no evil spirits were present. Garlic was also hung outside the doorways of houses, and used extensively in the kitchen, as it was thought to have strong purifying properties. The faith in the healing powers of garlic was so strong that ordinary people who had an aversion to garlic were thought of as highly suspect, and in some cases might even be persecuted as vampires themselves.

The vampire's sense of smell was so sensitive, it was thought, that it could detect the scent of a sleeping person's blood from a long way off, and make its way towards it using its nose as a guide. This idea, too, has some basis in the natural world, in that it may have been derived from observing the behaviour of animals. Many animals, including wolves, dogs, and certain species of bat, are able to sniff out a live animal or a corpse, follow its trail, and find it. Given that the vampire was conceived of as a creature which subsisted on the blood of live human beings, it is not surprising that people would imagine it to have a very refined sense of smell, and be able, like wolves and bats, to hunt down its victims.

In addition to its powerful sense of smell, the vampire was thought in some cultures to have enhanced vision, so that it could see and track victims in the dark, often from miles away. Once again, while this seems an entirely fanciful notion, it did have some basis of reality in nature. Owls, for example, have very strong night vision, allowing them to hunt in darkness.

Vampires were also thought to have a highly developed sense of hearing, rather like bats, whose sensitive ears help them to pinpoint their prey by means of echolocation. Vampire bats also have heat sensors, allowing them to sense blood near the surface of the victim's skin, and this may explain why in some versions of the legend, vampires can stalk their victims by means of infra-red heat sensors.

Super powers

In some versions of the mythology, vampires are able to turn themselves into bats, wolves, or other animals at will. Vampires may also become foxes, rats, and moths, or transform themselves into vapours, allowing them to slip through cracks under a door or a window. They are also, in some legends, able to vanish, or to live side by side with human beings as invisible presences. According to some tales, as they grow older, they become stronger, and can reach a point where their strength is that of ten men. They may also be able to travel very fast, at superhuman speeds,

that make it impossible to see them with the naked eye, or disappear from one place and appear in another.

Vampires are also said to be able to hypnotize their victims before attacking them. Their ability to do this depends on the victim's own strength of will. After the attack, vampires may hypnotize their victims to forget what happened.

Another bizarre feature of the vampire is their ability to withstand many forms of attack. They cannot be killed with knives, guns, or sticks. (An exception may be made if the gun is loaded with silver bullets, and in early times, a corpse might be shot through with a silver bullet to make sure the inhabitant was well and truly dead.) The only well-established way to eradicate vampires entirely, according to folklore, is to pierce them with a stake, cut out their hearts, cut off their heads, and burn their bodies to ashes. This is necessary because vampires, so we are told, regenerate themselves very quickly. If they are wounded, their injuries will heal overnight, and may do so even more quickly if they find a victim whose body they can drain entirely of blood.

Finally, in some versions of the legend, vampires are able to control the minds of nocturnal animals such as bats, mice, rats, and wolves. These animals act as slaves to their master, and they are so faithful to him that they may lay down their lives for him. Vampires may also control the weather, bringing a blanket of fog down to cover their traces, or blowing up a storm to prevent them being followed. Vampires also, by biting their victims, may create human slaves, who will do their bidding come what may.

Vampires & Immortality

Over the centuries, as we have discussed, the image of the vampire changed from that of a monstrous, bloated corpse stalking its victims out of revenge at having been excluded from the land of the living, into a svelte nobleman who charmed members of high society, especially rich women, with his pallid beauty, refined sensibilities, and deathly allure. By the late nineteenth century, the vampire had become largely a creature of literature and legend, and as remote rural communities began to feel the effects of modern life, there were few who genuinely still believed in the existence of real vampires. However, the myth still continued – and continues – to hold great fascination for many people in many cultures all over the world. One of the reasons for this is that it centres on the notion of immortality.

During the twentieth century, Christian belief in Europe gradually declined, and with it the conventional idea of life after death; thus the legend of the vampire, which involves the story of the 'undead' spirit, became an appealing way of continuing to reflect on the mysteries of the life hereafter, outside of a religious context.

Horrible stench

Descriptions of vampires in medieval times emphasized the horror of the monster's decomposing body, with lurid accounts of the blood running from its orifices, its swollen limbs, matted hair, long nails, and so on. As well as these less than attractive features, the medieval vampire emitted the most horrible stench, which could be smelt for miles, and could cause people to faint with disgust. Unlike his later counterpart, the sophisticated nobleman, the medieval vampire was a very realistic 'walking dead', in that its evil-smelling, rotting corpse was vividly described in every detail. It was also conceived of as a 'plague bringer'; it was thought that the stench could waft into houses and infect whole families, who would fall ill merely by breathing 'unclean' air.

Underlying these accounts was a well-grounded fear that corpses could spread disease, and must be buried in places away from human habitation in order to stop contagious illnesses spreading. Some commentators have noted that in times of plague, bodies were often buried in mass graves, which were visited by gravediggers again and again, and might be opened many times. These workmen would see bodies in various stages of decomposition, some of them with the features that so frightened medieval people – fat, swollen limbs, rosy cheeks, a ruddy complexion, long nails and hair, dark blood running out of the mouth, ears, and nose – and bring back tales of what they had seen. Thus, an extreme anxiety developed that corpses could come back to life, and if they did, they would spread the disease that they had died of – either through the foul, pestilential stench that they brought with them, or by their bloodsucking forays, attacking innocent sleeping victims.

'Eternal death'

In these early accounts, immortality was seen as a kind of curse – 'eternal death', the flip side of 'eternal life' as promised by the Christian priests. An important aspect of the vampire was that it could only sustain itself by sucking the blood of living beings, and ultimately causing their death by doing so. It was as if the pagan images of medieval culture, and of course the peasants' closeness to the ordinary phases of nature (including witnessing the dead and dying) combined to make a mockery of the Christian idea of 'eternal life' by conjuring up this monstrous being that could not die, yet lived a miserable half-life, preying on its victims at night and draining their lifeblood away from them as they slept.

Drinking the blood of Christ

The idea of drinking blood to attain eternal life is also at the heart of Christian ritual, in the celebration of mass. In the Eucharist, or Holy Communion, as it is also known, Christians who have been baptized and confirmed come up to the altar to take the bread and wine, which is conceived of as the body and blood of Christ. The priest first takes a chalice, holds it up and says: 'Drink ye all of this; for this is my Blood of the New Testament, which is shed for you and for many for the remission of sins; Do this, as oft as ye shall drink it, in remembrance of me.' Each communicant is then given a wafer of bread and a sip of wine from the same chalice.

Today, there is some controversy over the ritual of the Eucharist within the Christian church regarding the issue of what is called 'transubstantiation'. Some sects argue that the ritual is purely symbolic, an act of faith,

remembrance, and gratitude for Christ's self-sacrifice on the cross; others, including the Roman Catholic church, maintain that during the service, the wine and the bread actually turn into Christ's blood and body, and that communicants therefore drink his blood and eat his flesh.

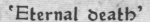

The quest for immortality

Whatever the status of these beliefs, it is clear that human beings through the centuries have always shown an immense urge to overcome death through belief in an afterlife, and through various ritualistic practices, many of which have included the drinking of blood. The early vampire myth, with its roots in the Slavic 'old religion' of 'undead' spirits and demons, is part of that quest. The nineteenth century vampire, which was the start of a nobly born, wealthy individual, has other cultural references (not least, as some political commentators have pointed out, a critique of the nobility, whose decadent, privileged lifestyle 'leeches' the morals of society, and the lifeblood of the lower orders). However, what seems to bind them all together is the common quest for immortality.

In the twentieth and twenty-first century, the image of the vampire as a seeker of immortality – whether visualized as a horrifying monster from the grave or a well-groomed aristocrat – has tended to be obscured. The camp horror elements of the legend have attracted many talented film-makers and fiction writers, who have created tremendously entertaining fantasies for a popular market, so much so that the more serious aspects of the stories have been somewhat overlooked. However, in more recent years, building on the important themes of human sexuality, death, and the quest for immortality that have been present in fictional accounts of vampirism

A female vampire from the 1970 film, *Count Yorga, Vampire*.

since the days of Bram Stoker's *Dracula*, there has been a revival of the myth; one recent example is Stephenie Meyer's vampire romance series *Twilight*, aimed at a teenage market (see page 164). Once again, the vampire legend shows itself able to accommodate a discussion of emotional issues that appeal to contemporary youth: for example, the feelings that many teenagers experience as they hit adolescence; that they are 'different' from others, 'weird', 'looking in from the outside', and so on. In addition, Meyer's books address the teenager's perennial preoccupation with the 'big questions', such as love, sex, death, and the aspiration to live for ever.

The female vampire

As we have noted, the medieval European image of the vampire as a mouldering corpse was a far from sexually attractive one. It is only during the Regency period, with John Polidori's *The Vampyre*, that we encounter the seductive vampire, in the person of Lord Ruthven, and then again in the Victorian period with the most famous vampire of them all, Bram Stoker's *Dracula*. One of the many reasons for the popularity of these stories was that they touched on the connection between sex and death: women who had sexual liaisons with vampires not only risked public shame and humiliation, they also risked being transformed into seductive sirens or dying. In Stoker's *Dracula*, the women could also become violent, even murderously so towards babies. To a repressed female readership nurtured on Victorian ideas of chastity, domesticity and selfless womanhood, these possibilities must have seemed horrifying – but in an erotic, exciting way.

Stoker drew on a deep vein of literature and folklore that conceived of the vampire as, among other incarnations, a beautiful, seductive woman who could suck the lifeblood out of a man, murder little children, and even eat them. These tales expressed deep fears about the power of female sexuality and fertility, and are present in many different cultures around the world. For example, the Ancient Greeks told of the beautiful Libyan Queen Lamia, who turned into a hideous child-eating demon, while the Mesapotamians feared Lilith, a highly seductive, serpentine evil spirit who appeared to men in erotic dreams (see page 75). In more modern tales of female vampires, the sexual elements of penetration (piercing the skin), and lust (sucking the blood) are clear; thus, these stories resurrect age-old anxieties about woman's ability to seduce and control men, and the possibility that this power may lead them to abandon their traditional roles as dutiful wives, mothers, and daughters.

In the same way, stories of lesbian vampires, such as Sheridan Le Fanu's novella *Carmilla* (see page 147) allowed readers to explore a taboo subject in a fantasy setting, thus circumventing the strict sexual mores of the time. Some critics believe that Le Fanu's novel was based on the historical figure of Countess Báthory, who was said to have murdered countless young women, bathing in their blood (see page 107). However, others believe that the story of Carmilla is more significant as a precursor than Bram Stoker's male protagonist, Count Dracula.

Whatever the truth, it seems that historically, the female vampire is a powerful mythical creation, expressing the fear of the sexually alluring woman as a dangerous threat to the patriarchal order.

CHAPTER 3

Myths and Legends

he dictionary definition of the vampire is 'a corpse that rises nightly from its grave to drink the blood of the living'. The belief in vampires arose in the medieval Slavic 'old religion' and then, in the centuries that followed, caught the imagination of writers, artists and film-makers, developing into the suave, sophisticated figure that we know today. Parallel to this European tradition are many other ancient belief systems across the globe that involve similar figures to the vampire: revenants who stalk the living, drinking their blood so as to sustain themselves in the shadowy afterlife.

The Strix

Ancient Greece, as we know, had a very highly developed belief system, with many complex myths surrounding the pantheon of gods that were worshipped. Among these, we find several tales about female demons, such as the storm demon Lamia, a woman who in life suffered the death of her children and took her revenge by preying on babies, stealing them away to suck their blood and eat their flesh (see page 72). Allied to this myth is the story of Lilith (see page 75), which comes from Hebrew mythology. In some ancient versions of this story, Lilith is the first wife of Adam who refuses to obey him, is banished from the Garden of Eden, and then returns in snake form to tempt him. She becomes an evil demon, seducing men and stealing infants away from their mothers, as well as bearing demon children herself who visit humankind and wreak havoc upon it. This myth endured for centuries, and right up until the eighteenth century, Lilith was held responsible for infant deaths, impotence, and infertility. Significantly, both Lamia and Lilith are women who are able to transform themselves into snakes, echoing another aspect of the vampire myth, which is the revenants' ability to assume non-human forms.

As well as these female demons, there are other ancient mythological creatures who share some characteristics with the vampire. One of these is the Strix, whose Latin name comes from the Greek word for owl. The Strix was a legendary figure from Ancient Roman culture, which was based on the European Scops owl. This small, insect-eating owl was feared as a creature of ill omen, and when it appeared at night, giving its characteristic low whistling call, it was thought that any human in the vicinity would experience death, either his or her own, or that of a loved one.

The Burney Relief, a Babylonian cult plaque of the demoness
Lilith, the first wife of Adam according to rabbinic tradition

The shape-shifting Strigoi

The legendary Strix differed from the Scops owl in that it was said to be a creature who drank the blood of human beings, and ate their flesh. The legend of the Strix is that their mother, Polyphonte, a companion of the goddess Artemis, fell in love with a wild bear and bore him two sons. These sons hunted human beings to survive, feeding on their flesh, and as a punishment, were turned into animals. One of them became a Strix, a nocturnal bird of ill-omen, and 'a harbinger of war and civil strife to men'. It was thought that the Strix disembowelled its victims, which could include human infants. Later, in medieval times, the Strix was reputed to be an evil female demon. In Romania, it gave its name to the *strigoi*, or vampire. In this version of the legend, the figure is the troubled soul of a dead person who has taken the form of a wild animal. In some cases, the strigoi could even be a living person with superpowers, such as the ability to transform him or herself into a shrieking bird.

Marrying a corpse

In Romanian folklore, a person could become a strigoi if he or she died before they were married. Bizarrely, in these cases, the corpse of the dead person might be married to another unmarried living person, in the belief that such a union could stop this from happening. However, in some cases, it was thought, the strigoi might return and try to have sexual intercourse with their former husband or wife. To avoid this possibility, the corpse of the unmarried person might be pierced with a stake, and the usual rites for dispelling vampires observed.

In addition, there were other specific remedies to discourage the corpse from changing shape and becoming a strigoi. One of these was to bury a bottle of wine at the graveside, dig it up a month or two later, and then drink it with the relatives of the deceased. Those who had drunk the wine, it was believed, would not be visited by the strigoi.

Thus it was that the mythological figure of the Strix, or night owl, that made its first appearance in the literature of Ancient Greece and Rome, migrated down the centuries into different cultures, becoming the strigoi of medieval Romanian folklore. As with the stories of bats and werewolves, ancient and medieval peoples observed the behaviour of the animals around them, especially those mysterious animals that were only seen at night, and built legends around them to explain their habits and explore their alien way of life. In this way, these animals played their part in the complex development of human civilization and its relationship to the natural world.

African vampires

Evil creatures who have morphed from human form into evil nocturnal birds are also a feature of non-European cultures. In West Africa, the Asanbosam, or Sasabonsam, is a legendary figure in the folklore of the Ashanti people. Myths about this creature occur in Ghana, Togo, and the Ivory Coast. The Asanbosam is a vampire-like animal that is said to live in trees and swoop down to attack people. Legend has it that this monster has iron claws and iron teeth, and preys on human beings and other animals, ripping them to shreds in order to drink their blood and devour their flesh.

Another blood-sucking creature from Ashanti folklore is the Obayifo. This is a kind of witch who is able to inhabit the body of a living human being. The Obayifo comes out at night, and is said to be visible by its luminous armpits and anus. It is always on the look-out for food, and is said to hang around the house when cooking is going on. It is believed to be able sometimes to enter the bodies of animals so as to attack human beings.

The Obayifo is particularly feared for its ability to suck the blood out of children from afar and also being able to draw the life force out of farm land so that it yields no harvest. It is thought to suck sap out of plants to assuage its thirst, and is often held responsible for diseases in crops. In cases of cocoa blight, for example, the Obayifo will be blamed. In order to combat the monster's destructive influence, an Okomfo, or witch doctor, will perform various rituals to banish it, and will be supported by the entire tribe in his endeavours. Among some African peoples, the Obayifo is known as the Asiman, and similar stories are told about its evil doings.

The Aboriginal Yara-ma-yha-who

In Australia, the mythical figure of the bloodsucking Yara-ma-yha-who would often be invoked by Aboriginal people to stop their children from wandering off on their own. This creature was said to be a small monkey or frog-like man with a large head, whose body was covered in red hair. Its face was dominated by a very wide mouth, and on the tips of its fingers and toes it had suckers like an octopus. It lived in trees, waiting for its victims to stop and rest in the shade, whereupon it would leap down to attack. Placing its suckers on the victim's skin, it would drain all the blood out of his or her body. It would then swallow the victim whole, wash down the meal with a drink from a nearby river, and then lie down to take a nap.

The next step of the story is a strange one, and demonstrates the gentle, humorous nature of much Aboriginal folklore. According to the legend, after a few hours the Yara-ma-yha-who would wake up and regurgitate its victim alive and unharmed. The only telltale sign of such an attack would be that the victim became a little shorter than before. If a person was attacked several times, he or she might also become a Yara-ma-yha-who, living in trees and waiting to attack innocent victims, especially children.

As has been pointed out by many commentators, the Yara-ma-yha-who is not strictly a vampire, since there is no suggestion that the creature is a revenant from the grave, or an undead soul of any sort; however, the blood-sucking behaviour of the Aboriginal sprite has much in common with the European tradition of the Strix and Strigoi, and with other folkloric sprites and demons from around the world, which have close parallels to the mythic tradition of the vampire.

The Female Demons

Ancient mythology is full of legends about female demons that prey on men and children. A recurring theme is that these demons have suffered barrenness in a former life, and so in the afterlife appear as a ghoul, taking their revenge by attacking children at night, while they are asleep, and devouring them. In many of the stories, the demons also seduce men, stealing them away from their wives, and sucking their blood, which helps to sustain their ghostly existence in the afterlife.

The Succubus

The parallels with vampires are obvious. Medieval folklore also contains accounts of the Succubus, a vampire-like creature who takes the form of a woman. The Succubus appears to a man at night, usually in a highly seductive form, and forces him to have repeated sexual intercourse with her, until he is drained of strength, or sometimes even dies. She may also feed on his blood, which is her way of taking his life force from him.

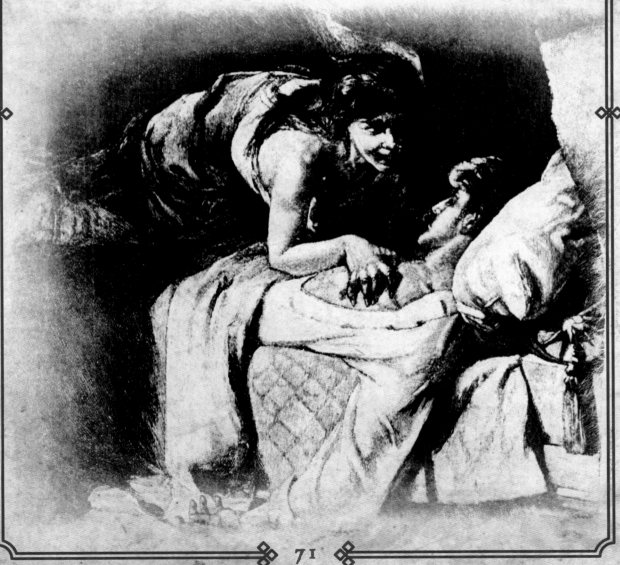

As with the tales of female vampires, what we encounter in the parallel myths and legends of such creatures is a universal anxiety about female sexuality. The fear is that if a woman fails to marry or to bear children in her lifetime, her jealousy will reach such proportions that, in the afterlife, she will reappear as a Succubus or Lamia, using her powerful feminine charms to corrupt other women's husbands, and destroying their offspring in revenge for her own barrenness.

Lamia the child eater

Lamia is a figure from Ancient Greek mythology, who appears in the writings of Diodorus Siculus, a historian from the first century BC. Diodorus recounts that Lamia was the daughter of King Belus of Egypt. In other accounts, she is reported to be the daughter of Poseidon, the god of the sea.

Whatever her provenance, her main claim to fame is that she had an affair with the god Zeus, bearing him several children. This apparently enraged Zeus's wife Hera to the point where she

murdered Lamia's children. In response, Lamia lost her mind and set off to wander the earth, preying on the children of other women, particularly newborn infants. She would attack them at night, carrying them off to a lonely place and devouring them. Diodorus reports that this vile habit distorted her face, so that instead of being a beautiful, young woman, she became a hideous hag. However, in other retellings of the myth, Lamia retains her beauty in the upper half of her body, while in the lower, she grows a penis, which she hides by draping a snakeskin around her loins.

With these often quite gruesome tales, the ancients conjured up the image of a woman who, denied the pleasures of motherhood, morphs into a man, adopting the violent, destructive qualities and aggressive sexual drives traditionally attributed to masculinity. Interestingly, in nearly all versions of the story, this unhappy state of affairs is initially occasioned by

another woman, the jealous Hera. It is Hera who condemns Lamia to a life of torment by murdering the illegitimate children she has borne as a result of her affair with Zeus. Much later, in Roman times, the poet Horace went further, suggesting that Hera may have actually forced Lamia to eat her own children, rather than simply murdering them. And there is also a legend that Hera cursed Lamia with the inability to close her eyes, so that she could find no rest, and was forever unable to dispel the vision of her dead children's faces from her consciousness.

Drinking infants' blood

In some accounts of the story, Zeus takes pity on Lamia and gives her the ability to take her eyes out, so that she will be able to rest. According to some sources, this also gives her the gift of prophecy. However, Lamia continues to live a nightmare existence, seemingly unable to stop herself from preying on sleeping infants and stealing them away to drink their blood and eat their flesh.

In the following centuries, the more sympathetic aspect of Lamia's history as a bereaved mother dropped away, and she became the personification of feminine vice. Instead of being a single historical figure, her name came to be interchangeable with that of the Succubus and the harlot, and she eventually became synonymous with any seductive woman with evil intent. She was depicted as a creature whose bare-breasted upper half took the alluring form of a beautiful woman, and whose lower half was that of a snake. This was a symbolic representation of her duplicity and hypocrisy, and once again, indicated the

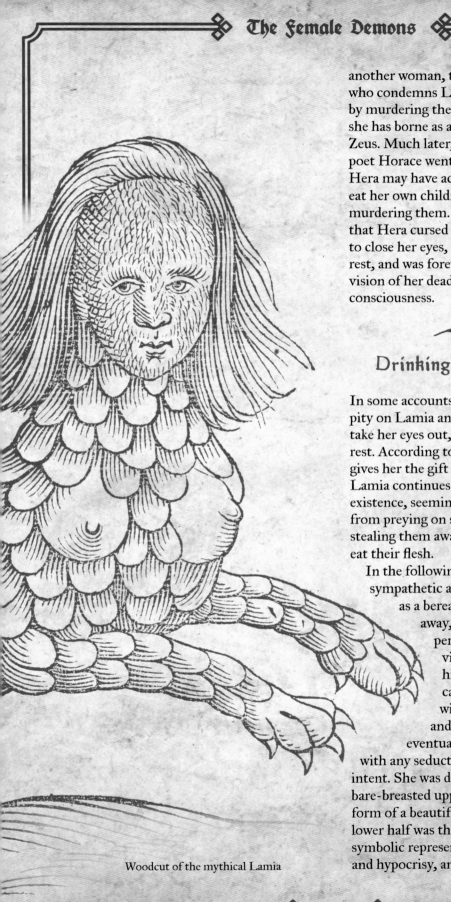

Woodcut of the mythical Lamia

fear that female sexuality, once freed from the bonds of motherhood and wifely duty, would prove a destructive, evil force to the rest of society.

Snake form

In 1819 the English poet John Keats wrote a narrative poem entitled *Lamia*, telling the story of how the god Hermes restores the serpentine Lamia to her human form. A Corinthian youth, Lycius, falls in love with her, and the couple are betrothed. At their wedding, however, a sage, Apollonius, reveals Lamia's true identity. She immediately reverts to her snake form, and the bridegroom promptly dies of grief. This poem did much to highlight the image of the Lamia in Victorian culture, and became one of Keats' most famous poems, chiming as it did with the repressive Victorian view of female sexuality.

Today, in modern Greece, the story of the Lamia still persists as part of the folklore of the country. Children are admonished that unless they behave, the dreaded Lamia will come to take them away. If an infant dies suddenly, in what we now call a cot death, the incident is sometimes described as being the result of strangulation by the Lamia. And if a woman

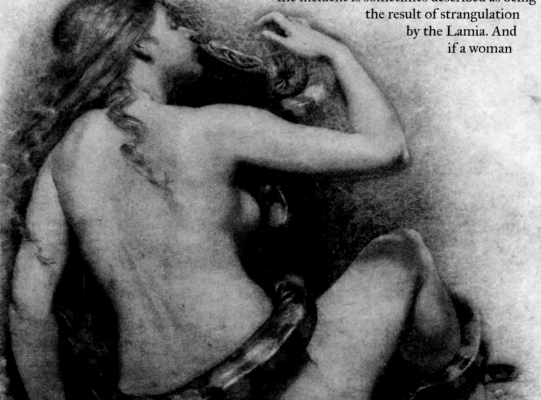

ABOVE AND ABOVE OPPOSITE: Painting of the classical myth *Lilith*, by Kenyon Cox.

fails to keep her house clean and tidy, her housework will be criticized as 'Lamia's sweeping'. Greedy or stupid women are also dubbed Lamia. Thus, in modern times, as well as in the past, the Lamia has become the symbol of all that is hated and feared in the figure of the unattached, undomesticated woman who has rejected motherhood.

The storm demon Lilith

Lilith, a snake-like character from Hebrew mythology briefly mentioned earlier, is very much akin to the Lamia, and as the centuries progress, the two become interchangeable. She began life in 4000 BC as one of several wind or storm demons in Mesopotamia. These demons were said to bring disease, illness, and death. Lilitu, as she was called, was a Succubus who appeared to men in their dreams, and was known for her lustful ways. It was believed that she caused men to have nocturnal emissions, thus draining away their strength. She was often depicted as having talons and wings, like a bird, and living in the desert. She would leave her lair at night, whenever a sandstorm blew up, to prey on men and generally wreak havoc with human lives.

Some believed she was the handmaiden of other deities, such as the Sumerian goddess of fertility, Inanna, and her Assyrian counterpart Ishtar; others, that she was an unclean woman or prostitute, a harbinger of death and disease.

The disobedient wife

There are many fascinating versions of the story in early Hebrew texts, some of which contradict the creation myth. In one story, the *Alphabet of Ben Sira*, Lilith appears as the first wife of Adam. When Adam demands that she lie beneath him during sexual intercourse, she refuses, saying that God created them both equal. She then flies off and consorts with demons, producing demonic children, one hundred of whom die every day. In other stories, such as those of the Kabbalah, Lilith herself turns into a serpent, and it is she who tempts Adam and Eve with the apple, causing their banishment from the Garden of Eden.

In the Middle Ages, Lilith was said to have married the King of Demons, Asmodeus, spreading chaos and misery at every opportunity. If a man became impotent, or a woman was found to be infertile, or a child died in infancy, Lilith would be blamed. Up until the eighteenth century, this superstition persisted: a magic circle would be drawn around the bedroom when a mother gave birth, and both mothers and babies would be given amulets to protect them. The names of the three angels who had tried to take her back to Adam – Sanvi, Sansanvi, and Semangelof – would also be invoked to keep her away.

Mother deity

Later, in the Romantic period, the German writer Goethe returned to the subject of Lilith in his great play *Faust*, characterizing her as a sorceress who suffocates men by winding her long hair tightly around them. In the Victorian period, the poet Robert Browning took a different approach, emphasizing that Lilith has an abject attachment to Adam, crawling like a snake to him and promising to be his slave.

In contemporary times, there has been a re-evaluation of Lilith. Some view her as an early mother goddess overseeing and celebrating an essentially feminine sphere of sexuality and fertility, on a par with positive nurturing deities such as the Egyptian goddess Isis. According to this view, the rise of patriarchy provoked a demonization of women, so that instead of being an essentially benevolent female force, Lilith becomes a destructive demon. Perhaps the most balanced way to view her, from our current perspective, is as a counterpart to such deities as the Indian goddess Kali, who has great sexual power that can be wielded for both positive or negative use. Significantly, this more subtle interpretation links with today's approach to the vampire myth, which stresses the creature's sympathetic, as well as destructive, aspects.

Eve and Lilith. Lilith tempting Eve with an apple in the Garden of Eden. Woodcut, German, 1470.

The Chupacabra

Unlike most of the mythical creatures described in this section, the Chupacabra is not part of ancient folklore. Rather, it is a monster of modern times, what we might describe, in contemporary terms, as an 'urban legend'. From the 1970s on, there were rumours of a goat-eating beast roaming the remote areas of the world and killing small animals, but reported sightings of this mysterious vampire-like animal reached their height in the 1990s. At this time, the Chupacabra, as it came to be called, was blamed for killing various kinds of livestock in many parts of the Americas, as far as Mexico in the south and Maine in the north.

To date, there has been no confirmed scientific evidence that such a monstrous creature exists. However, some animals have been seen (and in some cases shot, or their corpses found) and identified as aberrant types of coyote or dog. Nonetheless, in many communities, particularly those of Latin America, the Chupacabra continues to be feared as a horrifying monster that will attack smaller animals such as goats, emptying their entire bodies of blood.

The goat sucker

In Spanish, Chupacabra literally means 'sucker of goats'. The name has been attributed to Silverio Perez, a well-known TV host, comedian, and musician from Puerto Rico. He coined the term after seeing reports in the newspapers about the deaths of livestock and the suspicion that a vampire-like creature had been responsible for killing them. The name caught on, and today, it has become much used throughout the Americas.

In the early 1990s in Puerto Rico, there were rumours of a strange beast that had been seen in remote parts of the country. It was said to be a large, lumbering creature the size of a bear, with a row of spines along its entire back, from neck to tail. It also, according to some reports, had large, vicious-looking fangs. Other accounts described the animal as a reptile-like creature with leathery greenish-grey skin and quills running down its back. In other descriptions, the reptile's body was covered in scales.

The Chupacabra was thought to be a creature standing about one metre high with long back legs and shorter front ones. It hopped about like a kangaroo or dinosaur. Some reports alleged that when disturbed or frightened, it emitted a screeching noise, and also began to hiss. In addition, it left a revolting smell behind it, as of sulphur. Furthermore, its eyes glowed red in the dark, and could cause the onlooker to succumb to waves of nausea.

As well as being likened to a bear and a reptile, the Chupacabra was sometimes compared to a dog. In this description, it was a hairless wolf-like animal with deep eye sockets, large fangs, and claws. The characteristic spine of quills running down its back was also evident.

Bloodsucking vampire

In March 1995, eight sheep in Puerto Rico were found to have died. Each one of them reportedly had three puncture wounds near the neck and had been entirely drained of blood. Subsequently, near the town of Canovanas, around 150 farm animals met a similar fate. No one knew the reason why until an eyewitness named Madelyne Tolentino reported that she had seen a peculiar animal lurking in the street where she lived, watching her as she hung out her washing to dry. She and her husband tried to capture it, but it beat a hasty retreat. Another eyewitness, Michael Negron, also claimed to have seen the beast hopping about in the dirt outside his house. 'It was about three or four feet tall, with skin like that of a dinosaur,' he reported. 'It had eyes the size of hens' eggs, long fangs, and multicoloured spikes down its head and back'. Convinced that these reports were true, the mayor of the town, Jose Soto Rivera, mounted a hunt for the animal, but it was never found.

El Vampiro de Moca

Two decades before, in the town of Moca, there had been similar killings of livestock. These had been attributed to a vampire, named 'El Vampiro de Moca'. There had also been rumours that the livestock killed

were victims of a satanic cult. Each of the animals had been bled dry, through small incisions in the neck and chest area.

Not surprisingly, the new spate of killings near Canovanas renewed anxiety that there was an evil, vampire-like creature stalking the area, and that it was merely a matter of time before human victims, especially small children, would be targeted. As similar animal deaths began to be reported in other Latin American countries – including Honduras, the Dominican Republic, El Salvador, Peru, Argentina, Panama, Nicaragua, Bolivia, Brazil, Colombia, Chile, and Mexico – panic began to mount.

Suspected Chupacabra sighting.

The Elmendorf Beast

The next development to cause a stir was in July 2004, when a rancher named Devin McAnally in Elmendorf, Texas, shot an animal that he saw attacking his livestock. This time, the dead body of a supposed chupacabra was available for inspection, and the media rushed to cover the story.

The corpse did indeed look grotesque. It was that of an emaciated, hairless dog with leathery blue-grey skin, long ears, and large pointed teeth. There were also small scales on the skin. The corpse was promptly dubbed the Elmendorf Beast and taken to the laboratory for tests. Various speculative theories then emerged as to its provenance.

One scientific opinion claimed that this was a Mexican Hairless Dog, a breed that is naturally devoid of hair, and that the unfortunate animal had undergone profound changes in appearance as a result of malnourishment, sickness, and possibly congenital abnormalities sustained at birth. Others suspected that it was a hybrid animal, possibly a cross between a wolf and a coyote. There was also a theory that the dog was suffering from severe sarcoptic mange, which would have caused all its hair to fall out. There were even suggestions that the animal might have been created in a laboratory, as part of a government medical research programme, and that the animal had somehow escaped into the wild.

In order to gain a rational explanation of the animal's appearance, attempts were made to extract DNA from the corpse. The results showed that it was indeed some kind of dog. However, the corpse was too decayed for the tests to reveal more than that. Thus it was that the mystery was never resolved.

Whatever the truth that lay behind the mystery, it must be said that the pictures of the Elmendorf Beast's corpse showed it to look more like a forlorn mangy coyote than the terrifying predator imagined in stories of the Chupacabra. To further bolster this impression, not long after this incident, two similar corpses were picked up in Texas and discovered to be coyotes suffering from severe cases of mange.

Big fangs

But the Chupacabra panic was not over. A year later, reports began to come in from Central Russia, where dozens of turkeys and sheep had mysteriously been killed overnight. As with the sheep in Latin America, there were bite marks on their necks and chest, and they had been completely drained of blood.

Next, residents in rural areas of Maine in the US began to complain of similar attacks on chickens. In addition, several dogs were reported to have been mauled by a larger creature.

At this point, a clue to the mystery suddenly came up. Back in Texas, a woman named Phylis Canion, who had lost many chickens to the supposed beast over the years, came across three unusual animal corpses near the perimeter of her farm. She photographed the corpses and put one of the heads into her freezer for identification. Experts were called in to view it, but their opinions were divided. The state mammologist, John Young, deemed it to be a grey fox suffering from mange. But biologists who studied the corpse's DNA determined that it was a coyote. Yet, as many people pointed out, this beast was not like any coyote seen before. It had big fangs, grey-blue skin, and no hair.

In the years that followed there were other sightings from countries all over the world. In the Philippines, one farmer saw a dog-like animal attack his chickens, while once again in Texas, Brandon Riedel, a county deputy, filmed a hairless animal with a long snout loping along the back roads of the area. It had short front legs and long back ones. Once again, the animal was identified as a coyote, although it did seem very different from the rest of the species.

Today, the legend of the Chupacabra continues. Sightings are often reported, the creature being said to resemble many different animals, including rats, bats, kangaroos, and of course, hairless dogs. In some cases, there have been reports of the creature looking like a dinosaur.

The legend lives on

Not only this, there are also some theories that the Chupacabra may be a pet who has escaped from a race of aliens. Such creatures are known to UFO enthusiasts as 'Anomolous Biological Entities' or ABEs. It is argued that they have been created by alien beings who have developed ways of linking the genetic data of different organisms, creating hybrid creatures that may belong to extraterrestrial environments.

Not surprisingly, such theories are in general viewed with some scepticism. However, the persistent attacks on livestock, in which the animals are bitten at the chest and neck, and completely drained of blood, have to date still not been explained in a persuasive fashion. These continue to occur in different parts of the world, much to the consternation of farmers and rural dwellers in these areas.

Thus, until somebody comes up with a rational explanation for these mystifying attacks, the legend of the Chupacabra will continue to live on as one of the most intriguing urban myths of our time.

Psychology & Anthropology

One of the most ancient forms of female vampire is the Cihuateteo, a legendary figure from Aztec mythology. The Aztecs created a great and lasting empire from their heartland in Mexico up until the sixteenth century, when the area was colonized by the Spanish. Their spiritual, religious and artistic culture was highly developed and complex, and they worshipped a huge pantheon of gods, many of them conceived as extremely violent and hostile to human beings. As in many primitive cultures, these all-powerful gods needed to be propitiated, and sacrifices – including the sacrifice of human children – were made to them at different times of year to ensure their peaceful coexistence with the mortal world.

Among these deities was the Cihuateteo (also known as the Civateteo or Cihuateotl). She was the spirit of a woman who had died in childbirth. The Aztecs believed that giving birth to a child was a type of battle, in which the woman became a warrior. When a woman died in this way, she would be honoured as a fallen martyr, and worshipped accordingly.

Sexual misdeeds

However, the Cihuateteo's spirit was not a benign presence in the world, and in the afterlife, a victim of childbirth would go on to haunt the living. In particular, she would come out when the sun set in the west, and wait at crossroads in the darkness of night to attack her victims. She was known for her ability to seduce any man so that he left his wife and family and became her sexual slave. In addition, she was thought to steal young children away from their mothers, and cause whole families and communities to succumb to sickness and disease. In particular, if individuals suffered epileptic fits, or showed signs of mental illness, this would often be put down to the malign influence of the Cihuateteo.

The Cihuateteo was much feared throughout the region, and was thought to become particularly dangerous at certain times of year, when she would leave her home in the sky and come down to the human world to cause misery and chaos. In some Aztec belief systems, the Cihuateteo was thought to be an emissary from Mictlan, the lowest level of the underworld, where the dead lived. In others, she was believed to be the handmaiden of the goddess Tlazolteotl. Tlazolteotl was a deity believed to have a dual role: on the one hand, she presided over the world of filth, vice, and adultery, and on the other, she had the power to purify individuals from their sins and heal the ills, including disease and family strife, caused by their sexual misdeeds.

Altar of skeletons

We can see images of the Cihuateteo today in various sculptures that date from the Mesoamerican civilization. In some cases, she is represented as having the face of a skeleton. Sometimes, her head is decorated with a garland of skeletons, and she may have a necklace of human hands. She is also depicted on some occasions as having talons like a bird of prey instead of hands. Her mouth may be open, so as to suck the blood of young infants from them, or she may show rows of sharp teeth, with which to tear apart the blood of her victims. Often, she sits on an altar of human skeletons, as befits her position as emissary from the home of the dead.

It is fascinating to note the way in which similar images occur in the folklore of different regions, and at different periods in history, across the world. For example, in the legend of the Cihuateteo, we find many links with the mythology of the European vampire: for example, the idea of the revenant or ghost who has suffered in life, and who comes back to wreak revenge on the living. And there are other points of similarity in this ancient Aztec story: for instance, the idea of bloodsucking and flesh eating; of sexual seduction, to the point where the victims forget or deny their family ties; of the spreading of communicable diseases, often fatal ones; and of the revenant inhabiting the souls of the living, so that they become mad and lose their reason entirely. In addition, we find particular details that each civilization has in common, such as the idea that evil spirits haunt crossroads. These are ideas that appear to occur in mythologies across the world, regardless of cultural and religious divides.

Carl Jung's 'collective unconscious'

This similarity between the various folkloric cultures of the world was observed by the psychiatrist Carl Jung, a contemporary of Freud's. He built a theory around it, which he termed 'the collective unconscious'. According to this idea, all humanity shares 'a reservoir of the experiences of our species'

that is expressed in folklore, and in the archetypal figures within it, such as, in this instance, the bereaved mother. Just as Freud argued that each and every one of us has an unconscious (that is, a part of the mind that we are not fully aware of, and that drives our behaviour) Jung believed that the human race also shares a communal unconscious, which fuels the creation of folk tales, religion, and art. Freud himself did not share this belief in a collective unconscious, and the two psychoanalysts fell out over this and many other issues.

However, work in these fascinating fields continued, and soon particular images and figures from ancient folklore began to be discussed in the world of psychiatry. In the early part of the twentieth century, the figure of the vampire became the subject of an interesting correspondence between Sigmund Freud, the founder of psychoanalysis, and his British biographer and follower, Ernest Jones.

The psychology of vampirism

Freud had argued, though not in any great depth, that belief in 'hostile demons' has a psychological cause: namely, that when a beloved person dies, negative feelings towards them are repressed, and that these feelings come back to haunt the living – whether family, friends, or lovers – in dreams. Ernest Jones took up this theme in a groundbreaking essay on the vampire, published in German in 1912. He argued that the image of the vampire was a 'projection' – an embodiment of the living person's ambivalent feelings, both of hatred and love, towards the dead person. It is for this reason that the vampire is said to return to visit the home of its nearest relatives.

In addition, Jones maintained that the vampire 'belief complex', as he termed it, was a form of regression to an early infant state. This state he described as 'an infantile sadistic-masochistic phase of development' in which the young child expresses anger towards his parents, especially his mother, by biting. He argued that when the child grows up and the parent dies, he or she may begin to feel unconsciously guilty about these early hostile feelings (and others accrued along the way), and may therefore begin to 'project' these feelings onto the dead parent, imagining that the parent will come back in a hostile guise to wreak revenge.

In addition, he maintained that the mixture of emotions conjured up by the folkloric image of the vampire is expressed by the 'sucking' aspect of the child's experience, which symbolizes love, and nurturing; and that furthermore, there is a 'biting' aspect, which represents hatred, or at any rate some kind of destructive, violent impulse.

Oral fixation: sucking and biting

This argument may perhaps seem tortuous, but in later studies on the psychology of sexuality, psychoanalysts such as Karl Abraham and Melanie Klein took up the theme of Jones' early paper on the vampire. In their descriptions of infant development, they discussed the way that, once the baby's teeth come through, it begins to find pleasure not just from sucking at its mother's breast, but from biting it as well. (It is often, at this stage, when the biting becomes excessive, that the mother will understandably decide to wean the baby.) Depending on how successfully the baby and mother negotiate these important developmental stages, the infant will mature normally, or become fixated, to a lesser or greater degree, at the oral stage. This kind of fixation leads to various types of unhealthily

rigid personality traits, mental imbalance, or, in the worst case, severe psychological illness.

Thus, according to this psychological reading, the vampire stands as a representation of humanity's fixation on the primitive oral stage of development, in which pleasure is received by sucking, biting, chewing, and so on. Our interest in, and excitement about, vampires, is to do with this early memory of infancy, and may also be an attempt to overcome the ambiguities occasioned by such powerful, contradictory emotions.

Whether or not we accept this explanation, it does seem likely that the figure of the vampire embodies some of our darkest fears and desires: firstly, our anxieties about our possible hostile feelings to those who have gone before us, especially parents and family relatives; and secondly, our primitive urge to return to the oral stage, in which sucking and biting are a childish source of pleasure.

The Aswang

These intellectual adventures into the primitive world of ancient folklore, pointing out recurring cross-cultural images, were exciting developments in several fields, from psychology to anthropology. While psychoanalysts studied the meaning of folkloric figures in terms of individual psychology, cultural anthropologists began to see links between the myths and legends of many different cultures around the world. And none appeared to recur more frequently than the figure of the bloodsucking revenant or vampire.

Today, many of these myths and legends continue to persist, particularly in parts of the world where folklore still plays a major part in people's lives. In the Philippines today, the female figure of the Aswang, a shapeshifting vampire, continues to be feared. This mythical creature is an old woman who takes the form of an animal at night – sometimes a bat, sometimes a creature with a long nose – and hunts down victims to eat. The Aswang is able to suck a foetus out of its mother's womb, steal a baby from its cradle, and take it home to eat. The Aswang is said to be particularly partial to hearts and livers. In some cases, the Aswang may replace its victim with a phoney baby or child, which will become ill and die. By day, the Aswang can be recognized by its bloodshot eyes, which are caused by having to stay up all night, searching for victims.

As in so many cultures, this female demon is blamed for causing all sorts of ills, particularly miscarriage and early death in infants. It is known across the Philippines by several different names, including the 'tik-tik' and 'wak wak'. Other related revenant figures from the region include the Manananggal, a bat-like witch who is able to split its body in half, and which devours human beings. Interestingly, both the Aswang and the Manananggal are said to dislike garlic. There are also thought to be particular ways of telling whether a person is an Aswang or Manananggal, such as by bending over and looking at it with the head between the legs, or by seeing a reflection of oneself in their eyes. In addition, there are said to be specific ways of warding off such creatures, for example throwing salt at them, which burns their skin. Significantly, the Manananggal, like the European vampire, is believed to hate sunlight and to be afraid of silver weapons. Whether this idea was introduced from Europe, or

Suspected sighting of the Manananggal.

whether Europeans took it over from the East, remains a mystery.

Similar to the Filipino Aswang is the Soucouyant of Trinidadian folklore, an old hag who can change shape, shedding her skin to become a fireball that flies through the air at night. The Soucouyant sucks blood from her victims, who may die and become Soucoyants as well. As with the European vampire, the Soucouyant can be repelled by scattering grains of rice on the ground, so that she must count them all; alternatively, salt can be sprinkled on the place where she left her skin, so that she will burn to death when she puts it back on.

The Vetala

From Hindu mythology comes the Vetala, also known as the Baital. This is an evil spirit that haunts cemeteries and enters corpses. It may continue to inhabit the corpse or leave it to cause trouble for the human world.

Its specialities are causing miscarriages, sending people mad, or killing children. However, it may also be a force for good on certain occasions, since it can guard villages from attack.

The Vetala inhabits a mysterious world somewhere between the living and the dead, and has lived for many centuries. Its vast store of knowledge, experience, and insight make it attractive to witches and sorcerers, who often try to capture and enslave it. However, it is a clever spirit, and knows how to escape capture. In one legend, King Vikramaditya, who lived in the first century BC, tried to capture a Vetala that lived in a tree in a graveyard. The only way to catch the Vetala was to remain silent, come what may. Once caught, the Vetala responded by telling the king stories, which so interested the king that he asked questions, whereupon the spell was broken and the Vetala returned

to his tree home. The stories that the Vetala told the king are collected in a book, the *Baital Pachisi*, a set of tales comparable to the *Arabian Nights*.

Also from Hindu mythology comes the Churel, an ugly old woman with a long, thick, black tongue which she uses to suck the blood from living mortals. The Churel is said to be the wandering spirit of a woman who has died in childbirth. She begins her spirit life by sucking the blood from her former husband, and continues to seek out young men as victims, living by streams and rivers, and lying in wait for them.

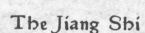

The Jiang Shi

Jiang Shi are Chinese vampires. According to legend, they come into being when a dead person's soul refuses to leave its body, and go on to cause trouble to the living. They have the appearance of decomposing corpses, with a horrible, furry green skin and long white hair. In ancient mythology, they sucked the essence of life from human beings, but in more recent times – possibly because of the influence of western stories about vampires – they are believed to suck blood from the living. A defining feature of the Jiang Shi is its curious hopping gait. This feature is said to come from the ancient Chinese custom of transporting corpses of people who had died back to their hometowns. The corpses would be put on long bamboo sticks, which would bend up and down, making them look as though they were hopping. The list of vampire-like creatures from myths and legends in different countries and cultures is a long one, and it is not possible to mention them all here. However, what continues to fascinate those with an interest in folklore is that the figure of the vampire, or bloodsucking revenant, is a perennial one that occurs across many cultures, both ancient and modern.

CHAPTER 4

Vampire Devotees

In most people's minds, the vampire is a mythical entity, a figure that combines elements of ancient pagan beliefs and superstitions with playful modern-day romance and horror narratives. However, there are some who take the legend more seriously, to the extent of pursuing a vampiric lifestyle. This may simply involve looking the part, that is, wearing black clothes and ghoulish make-up, and identifying with what has become known as the 'goth' subculture. In some cases the fascination may be deeper, indicating serious psychological disturbance, and involving gruesome rituals such as the drinking of blood, or even necrophilia.

In this chapter we look at real-life vampires, beginning with an in-depth account of those infamous, bloodthirsty characters from history on whom the vampire myth is based: Vlad the Impaler, Elizabeth Báthory, and Gilles de Rais. We then move on to discuss some of the early serial killers who were dubbed vampires in their time: in particular, Fritz Haarman and Peter Kürten, who were at large in Germany in the 1920s and 1930s. During this period, the term 'serial killer' was not in common use; thus, the senseless, repeated murders perpetrated by these bloodthirsty individuals were attributed to vampirism, showing how even in the twentieth century, superstition and pagan belief were still rife.

Sava Savanović

The fear of crazed murderers who kill from bloodlust goes back centuries, and is a recurring theme in the history and culture of many northern European countries. One of the earliest serial killers said to be a vampire was the legend of Serbian Sava Savanović, who was said to have lived in an old watermill on the River Rogagica near a village called Zarozje. According to local legend, he preyed on millers who came to the watermill to grind their grain. Little more is known about him, except that the watermill, owned by the Jagodic family, continued to function until the 1950s, when it closed. Apparently, tourists today still come to see 'the vampire's mill'.

A so-called vampire who received a great deal of notoriety was Peter Plogojowitz, also known by his Serbian name Petar

Blagojevic. Plogojowitz was a Serbian peasant who would have lived out his life in obscurity except that when he died, in 1725, there was an outbreak of disease and death in his village, Kisilova. Within a matter of days, nine more people had died, after falling ill and rapidly deteriorating. Some of the victims told stories on their deathbeds that Plogojowitz had returned from the grave to try to strangle them. Plogojowitz's wife complained that his ghost visited her at night, demanding that she give him his shoes. She was so frightened by this that she moved to another village, but there was worse to come.

Killing of son

One night, according to the villagers, Peter Plogojowitz appeared to his son, asking for food. When the son demurred, his father promptly killed him, brutally and in cold blood. At this, the villagers decided it was time to dig up the errant vampire, and set out to the churchyard with the local priest, armed with spades, garlic, and a wooden stake. Also among the party was an official from the Austrian government, then ruling that part of Serbia, who went by the name of

Imperial Provisor Frombald.

When the body was dug up, Frombald was surprised to see that it looked strangely alive, as though it had been thriving underground. Its hair and beard had grown long, together with its fingernails, which looked new and young. Its cheeks were ruddy, and there appeared to be fresh blood emanating from its mouth. In a great state of agitation, the priest and villagers ran a wooden stake through the corpse's heart, at which point more rich, dark blood flowed from its ears and mouth. Taking this to be fresh blood, the assembled company panicked, and burned the body to ashes.

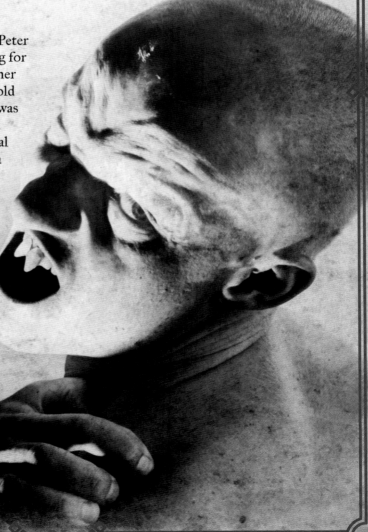

Vampire panic

In great distress, Frombald submitted a report of these doings to his superiors, hoping that he would not be castigated for taking part in such godless rituals. He was not, but the report was widely circulated and published in a national newspaper in Austria, fuelling a 'vampire panic' that spread to Germany, France and England. (For more information on this, see Chapter 1.)

At the time, there were various scientific refutations of the phenomenon, including explanations of what we know today.

There were also theories about communicable diseases playing a part in the quick succession of sudden deaths within a village or small town. One commentator, Michael Ranft, put the deaths down to anxiety provoked by the situation. He wrote: 'Sudden death gives rise to inquietude in the familiar circle. Inquietude has sorrow as a companion. Sorrow brings melancholy. Melancholy engenders restless nights and tormenting dreams. These dreams enfeeble body and spirit until illness overcomes, and eventually, death.' However, these arguments were dismissed by the superstitious villagers, and even today in the region the belief in vampires still persists.

Arnold Paole

Another instance of vampire panic came with the death of an outlaw called Arnold Paole, who died after falling off a haywagon in 1726. Not long afterwards, several people in the vicinity died suddenly, having complained that Paole had visited them at night. (Paole himself, during his life, had also mentioned that he had been plagued by a vampire, but had resolved the situation by eating earth from the vampire's grave and drinking his blood.)

Vampire panic was sweeping across Europe

Once again, the villagers decided to open up his grave, in the company of the local priest and government official, and were horrified to find the corpse looking healthy and swollen with blood. Paole and his four victims received the wooden stake treatment, and the episode contributed to the terror panic already sweeping across Europe by this time. Five years later, there was another outbreak of hysteria following the deaths of dozens of people from the same area in a matter of months, and the corpses were subjected to a number of anti-vampire rituals, including having their heads cut off and being burned to ashes.

Mercy Brown

At various times in history, there have been vampire panics occasioned by sudden deaths within a small community, following the burial of a local person. In the late nineteenth century, a family in Exeter, Rhode Island, suffered an outbreak of tuberculosis. The first to die was the mother of the family, Mary Brown, followed by her eldest daughter, also called Mary. Next came Mercy, a younger daughter, who died in 1892. The spate of deaths raised suspicions that a vampire was at work, so the father, George Brown, had the bodies

exhumed. While the corpses of the mother and eldest daughter had decomposed, Mercy appeared unchanged. In accordance with local superstitions, Mercy's heart was taken from her body, burned, and the ashes mixed with water. The solution was given to her brother Edwin to drink. Edwin, who was already ill, died two months afterwards.

The Highgate vampire

Today, urban myths and legends about vampires stalking graveyards still exist. One such instance was the media sensation surrounding the alleged Highgate Vampire, a revenant that supposedly inhabited the north London cemetery where Karl Marx and other well-known figures are buried. The story was promoted by a group of young occultists who roamed the cemetery in the 1960s, when it had been left untended for many years. They reported seeing a 'grey figure' and several ghosts, variously described as a cyclist, a woman wearing a white gown, and a tall man in a hat. There were also reports of bells ringing, and soft voices calling.

The local newspaper, not surprisingly, published several articles on this phenomenon, including a sighting of 'a King Vampire of the Undead', who was said to be a medieval nobleman. This man had apparently practised the black arts and had travelled from Wallachia to England in a coffin during the eighteenth century. In addition, foxes with throat wounds, whose bodies had been drained of blood, were

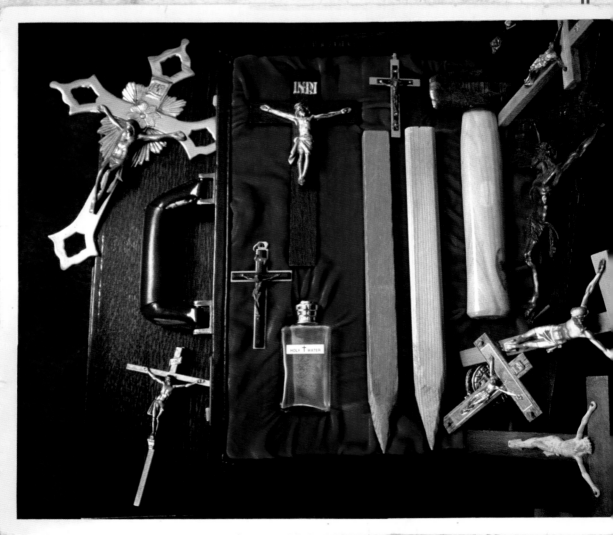

A vampire slayer's kit at Sean Manchester's house, England.

reported to have been seen lying around the cemetery.

A much publicized 'vampire hunt' then ensued, led by two local men, David Farrant and Sean Manchester. The pair offered claims and counter-claims as to the supernatural goings-on in the churchyard, until Farrant was jailed, in 1974, for vandalism and desecration of graves. He claimed that these crimes had been committed by satanists. Manchester later wrote a book on the subject entitled *The Highgate Vampire*. Today, the feud between the two men continues, each claiming to tell the definitive story of what remains an urban legend.

The Brummy vampire

Other urban areas in Britain have also yielded tales of vampirism, including an area of Birmingham known as Ward End. The stories began in 1981 when stones were thrown at houses in the area during the night. Although police set up infra-red cameras to survey the streets there, no human beings were ever seen. In 2004, reports came in that a man had been biting people. The local hospital and police station were not alerted, however, and there was no trace of the victims. In the end, in the absence of hard information about the so-called 'Brummy vampire', the case was dismissed as an urban legend, and the short-lived panic surrounding it subsided.

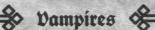

Richard Trenton Chase

It would be reassuring to imagine that all tales of vampirism in our time are the product of myth and superstition, and have no basis in reality. This usually appears to be so, as in the cases of the Highgate vampire and the Brummy vampire. Sadly, however, there continue to be instances of real vampirism, that is, dreadful crimes committed by extremely deranged individuals who believe themselves to be vampires and who act accordingly; murdering innocent victims at random to eat their flesh and drink their blood.

One such was Richard Trenton Chase, a serial killer from the city of Sacramento, California. Between 1977 and 1978 he killed six victims, drinking their blood and eating parts of their bodies. When he was caught, it emerged that he was seriously deluded. Under interrogation, he said he believed that Nazis were plotting his death by planting a certain kind of poison underneath his soap dish, which would turn his blood to powder.

Chase was born on 23 May 1950 in Santa Clara County, California. His parents split when he was a child and by all accounts, his early years were difficult. By the time he was an adolescent, he was abusing drugs and alcohol. During this time, he visited a psychiatrist complaining of sexual impotence. The psychiatrist diagnosed that he was suffering from repressed anger, but nothing further was done to improve the situation, and Chase went on to exhibit increasingly bizarre behaviour.

Rabbit blood

After leaving home in the belief that his mother was trying to poison him, he rented an apartment with college friends. He alarmed them by holding oranges to his head, thinking that the vitamin C would enter it that way. Other strange behaviour included shaving his head so that he could see how his bones 'moved around', and reporting that someone had stolen one of his arteries. He was frequently high on a cocktail of drugs and took to walking around the apartment naked. One by one, the friends moved out, until he was left there alone.

He then began to catch small animals, kill them, and eat them raw. In some cases, he mixed their organs in a blender with Coca Cola and drank them. He believed that, like a vampire, this would prolong his life, preventing his heart from shrinking. Not surprisingly, before long, he became ill and was admitted to hospital after injecting rabbit's blood into his veins and contracting blood poisoning. In hospital, he was nicknamed Dracula after being found with the remains of a small bird smeared over his mouth. He was treated for schizophrenia and drug-induced psychosis, and released into the care of his mother. Not long afterwards, his mother took him off his medication. That was when the nightmare began.

Hideous crimes

Chase went on a rampage lasting almost a year, killing a total of six innocent people. He began with a 51-year-old engineer, Ambrose Griffin, shooting him with a rifle. Next he shot Teresa Wallin, who was three months pregnant, mutilating and fornicating with her corpse before bathing in her blood. He then visited 38-year-old Evelyn Miroth, killing her, her six-year-old son Jason, her baby nephew David, and her friend Danny Meredith. After engaging in his usual necrophiliac and cannibalistic activities, he ran off to his apartment, where he drank the baby's blood, ate parts of his brain and other organs, before leaving the body in a churchyard.

Insanity plea

It was not long before police caught up with him. His apartment was full of gruesome evidence of his hideous activities, but he maintained his innocence, telling police that he had merely killed some dogs. Fortunately, the police did not believe him and he was arrested. At his trial in 1979, despite an insanity plea, he was found guilty of first degree murder on six counts and sentenced to death. A year later, while awaiting his fate, he committed suicide, overdosing on a hoard of anti-depressants prescribed to him by the prison doctor.

In recent times there have been other reports of murderers who believed themselves to be vampires, such as the case of Manuela and Daniel Ruda, who killed their friend Frank Hackert 'for Satan',

drank his blood, and then had sex in a coffin. They both denied having any personal responsibility for the murder. At their trial, they were declared to be suffering severe personality disorders, and were sentenced to be held in secure psychiatric units.

Unfortunately, these are not isolated instances. One of the most disturbing aspects of the Ruda case was that the couple received a great deal of fan mail from vampire enthusiasts. Today, there is speculation that the satanic cult of the vampire is increasing, especially in economically depressed areas where serious mental illness, especially among the young, can go untreated. Thankfully, however, the cases in which individuals believing themselves to be vampires actually commit murder, continue to be relatively few.

Vlad the Impaler

Vlad the Impaler, or Dracula, as he was also known, was a fifteenth-century Romanian prince who has gone down in history as one of the most bloodthirsty rulers of all time. His preferred method of torture was to impale his victims on a sharpened wooden stake, not only ensuring them a slow, agonizing death, but also encouraging onlookers, both soldiers and civilians, to surrender immediately to his troops. He was utterly ruthless in his desire to dominate, and stories of his cruel treatment towards mothers and children, as well as adult men, abound.

Devil worshipper?

There is no doubt that Vlad was an extremely barbaric ruler, but some believe that the stories about him being an insane devil worshipper and sadist, who revelled in his bloodthirsty crimes, are exaggerated. It is certainly true that his many enemies, especially those among the supporters of the Ottoman Empire which sought to rule Romania at the time, feared and hated him. He is reputed to have impaled thousands of ordinary men, women and children, in the course of war, or for any kind of resistance to his draconian edicts. However, among his own people, he was revered as a courageous freedom fighter, who for decades defended his country against the Turks. Be that as it may, his reputation as a mass murderer gave rise to many legends and myths, and his name, if not his actual historical existence, inspired Bram Stoker's novel *Dracula*, written many centuries later.

The son of the devil

Vlad the Impaler is thought to have been born in the city of Sighisoara, which is now in Romania but in those days was part of Transylvania. He was the second son of a Wallachian Prince, Vlad 'Dracul', who was living there in exile from his native land at the time. Vlad 'Dracul' was a warlord who had been initiated into a royal society, the 'Order of the Dragon', which accounted for his nickname, 'Dracul'. Significantly, in medieval times, the dragon was synonymous with the devil, and in the Romanian language, the word 'Dracul' also means 'devil'. Vlad Dracul's son became known as Dracula, meaning 'son of the dragon' – in other words, son of the devil. He certainly lived up to his name, as history recounts.

Vengeance for the past

Vlad 'Dracul' and his family were being hounded by the Ottoman sultan, forced to work for him as vassals, and to live in exile away from their homeland. In addition, Vlad was made to surrender two of his sons as hostages. Another son, little Vlad's older brother, was put to death in the most agonizing way, blinded with iron stakes and buried alive by his enemies. Not surprisingly, Vlad the younger grew up with an intense hatred of the Turks, and also of the boyars, high-ranking Russian, Moldavian, and Wallachian aristocrats who were often disloyal and competitive towards Vlad 'Dracul' and his family.

When young Vlad's father was finally assassinated in 1447, the years of waiting were over, and his turn came to rule. He resolved to do so with a vengeance, paying his enemies back for all the humiliations the family had suffered in the past.

The impalements begin

Vlad Dracula assembled an army and fought the Ottomans, invading Wallachia (now Romania) and managing to gain back control there. Despite his hideously barbaric methods of fighting, he was feted by his people, having ousted the Ottomans and once more taken up the throne in his native land. However, he still had a Herculean task to accomplish. After many years of misrule, Wallachia was a miserable, poverty-stricken country where the economy had completely collapsed and crime was endemic. Vlad set about restoring order, which meant, first and foremost, wiping out any possible threats to his power. To curb the boyars, he knighted lowly individuals and appointed them to important positions in the government. He also cut off trade between the boyars and the Saxons who had settled in Transylvania. When the boyars resisted, he responded by having Saxon officials in the city of Kronstadt impaled, as a warning to others not to flout his authority. Vlad was equally hostile towards other royal Romanian clans, capturing and murdering two of their princes, and murdering ordinary citizens who had sheltered them. There were stories that thousands of citizens had been impaled, earning the new ruler the nickname of Vlad Tepes – Vlad the Impaler; but although there was undoubtedly some truth in these accounts, it seems that the numbers were exaggerated by his many enemies.

Mass murderer

Whatever the truth of the matter, there is no doubt that by now, Vlad was gaining a reputation as a ruthless, bloodthirsty fighter. In 1461, having made an alliance with the Hungarians, he marched into Ottoman territory south of the Danube and laid waste to the population there. He later boasted that he had killed over 20,000 Turks and Bulgarians, burning them alive in their houses and chopping off their heads.

Not surprisingly, the Ottoman sultan responded by sending a huge army of 90,000 men to fight back. Nothing could have prepared the soldiers for what happened when they arrived at the region to do battle. They were greeted by the sight of thousands of dead and dying Turkish prisoners impaled on stakes, ranged across the countryside like a gruesome human forest. Dracula's reputation as a mass murderer was sealed, and from this time on, he was feared across Europe as a man who would stop at nothing to retain his power and position.

Vlad's wife commits suicide

However, ruthless as he was, Vlad's army was no match for the might of the Ottoman Empire, and the Turks eventually marched into Romania and attacked his castle. During the siege of the castle, his wife threw herself from a tower into the river below, vowing that she would rather have her body rot in the water and be eaten by the fish than fall captive to the Turks. When the castle was taken, the sultan threw Vlad into prison, and put his half-brother, the more compliant Radu the Handsome, on the throne of Wallachia.

Vlad languished in prison for a time – there is some dispute as to how

Impalement scene from a fifteenth-century German pamphlet
published by Matthias Hupnuff in Strasbourg

long for – but, by forging further alliances with the Hungarian crown, he was finally released. He converted to Catholicism and married a Hungarian countess, with whom he had two sons, and set about reconquering his native land, enthusiastically supported by his countrymen. In 1476, he was killed fighting near Bucharest. Afterwards, the Turkish soldiers cut off his head and sent it to the sultan, who displayed it prominently in Istanbul – fittingly enough, on a stake.

Reign of terror

But the legend of Vlad the Impaler lived on. Stories of the atrocities he had committed during his reign of terror, on a hitherto unprecedented scale involving thousands of victims, continued to horrify Western Europe. He was alleged to have killed between 40,000 and 100,000 people during his campaigns, mostly by impaling them, and to have razed whole villages to the ground, burning thousands more innocent victims in their houses. However, in Eastern Europe, particularly in Romania, where he was regarded as a freedom fighter and a hero, these figures were said to be exaggerated.

Statue of Vlad the Impaler (Dracula)
Tirgoviste Park, Wallachia, Romania

Red-hot iron stakes

The nature of the killings is also under dispute. In Germany, Vlad was alleged to be an insane sadist, whose crimes included burning, skinning, roasting, boiling, and drowning victims; forcing their relatives to eat their flesh; cutting off their limbs; nailing their hats to their heads; and torturing children and babies. He was particularly ferocious towards women, being apparently extremely concerned with female chastity. There are accounts that unmarried or adulterous women had their breasts and sexual organs cut out, and that they were impaled through the vagina with red-hot stakes. Merchants and workmen who cheated their customers, as well as common thieves, were also impaled, their bodies left out in the streets as a warning to others.

Deranged sadist?

Today, many historians believe that these accounts were sensationalized. The tales were circulated in manuscript form in the fifteenth century, and with the invention of the printing press, became bestsellers. They undoubtedly had a political purpose, to set the German public against the Romanians. This was not surprising, since Vlad had shown great cruelty towards the Saxons in the past. In addition, the Hungarian king, Corvinus, had reason to blacken Dracula's name. Corvinus needed to justify his failure to go to war with the Turks, so he accused Vlad of secretly supporting the Ottoman sultan, along with many other negative stories, making him a scapegoat for his own cowardice.

But, as the old saying goes, there's no smoke without fire. Vlad may not have been quite the deranged sadist that these stories made him out to be, but there is no doubt that he killed a large numbers of victims, often quite unnecessarily, and that impalement, a hideously painful form of torture and murder, was his preferred *modus operandi*.

Slow death

Vlad perfected a method of impalement to create maximum pain before death. A large wooden stake would be sharpened and oiled. It was important not to sharpen the stake too much, otherwise the victim would die of shock immediately after the stake was forced into the body. The stake would then be inserted into the victim's body through the anus, and forced right through until it came out of the victim's mouth. In certain cases, the stake would be inserted into other bodily orifices, or pushed through the stomach or chest.

The victim would then be left outside to die a slow, agonizing death, in full view of passers-by. The process could go on for hours, or even days. Sometimes, the victim would be hung upside down. The height of the stake would indicate the person's rank, and stakes would also be arranged in patterns, often around a village, town, or city that soldiers were targeting. Once the victim died, the body would be left on the stake, to rot away.

Count Dracula

While the bloodthirsty crimes of Vlad the Impaler have gone down in history, there is no suggestion that he himself drank blood, or was thought to be a vampire. However, as Dracula, son of the ferocious Vlad Dracul, he gave his name to the most famous fictional vampire of all time, Bram Stoker's Count Dracula.

> # THE VICTIM WOULD THEN BE LEFT OUTSIDE TO DIE A SLOW, AGONIZING DEATH

How did this come about? In the story by Bram Stoker, Count Dracula lives in the 'cursed land' of Transylvania. The author's original intention had, by all accounts, been to set the novel in Styria, a region of Austria. He had been inspired to do so by reading a book about a remote castle in the area, *Schloss Hainfeld, or a Winter in Lower Styria* by Captain Basil Hall, a noted British naval officer, traveller, and author. However, he then went on to read another book, entitled *Transylvanian Superstitions* by Emily Gerard, the Scottish wife of a Hungarian cavalryman. This was an account of the folklore of the forests in the region, telling of ruined castles, werewolves, and occult happenings. Gerard reported the local peasants' belief in Nosferatu, the vampire who returned from the grave to prey on the living, and told of how they tried to ward off evil by hanging garlic over their front doors. This seemed to be fertile territory for a horror story, and thus Stoker decided to change his mind, and set his tale in the remote woodlands of Transylvania.

Stoker was also influenced by another important work of the period, *An Account of the Principalities of Wallachia* and *Moldavia* by one William Wilkinson, published in 1820. It is known that Stoker made notes on this book, using it to sketch out the background for his story. In this work, he found out about the principalities of Moldavia, Transylvania, and Wallachia (now Romania), and came across the story of the notorious fifteenth-century prince, Vlad Dracul, and his son, Vlad Dracula. Stoker may also have heard about Vlad Dracula from his friend Armin Vambery, a Hungarian professor who was familiar with the history of the region. Whatever the case, the story of the crazed, evil Dragon Prince with a lust for blood piqued Stoker's interest, and the vampire Count Dracula was born.

The Bloodthirsty Countess

In recent times, some literary critics have questioned the idea that Stoker based his Count Dracula on Vlad the Impaler. They point instead to the legends surrounding Elizabeth Báthory, a sixteenth-century Countess who sexually abused, tortured, and murdered scores of young women servants at her remote castle, allegedly bathing in their blood to keep her skin looking young (see page 107).

The most likely scenario seems to be that Stoker, like any other fiction writer, drew inspiration from many sources, taking details from both history and legend to create a vivid romance of his own. It seems that he borrowed the name of Count Dracula for his tale, substituting it for the original name he had chosen for his protagonist, Count Wampyr. Other aspects of Dracula's history, such as his fondness for impaling his victims on stakes, were left out, possibly because Stoker did not know very much about them. Certainly, by choosing to set his story in the remote forests of Transylvania, Stoker mined a rich seam of folklore and peasant superstition in the region.

Dracula's castle

Today, after the fall of Communism in Romania, the connection between Stoker's Count Dracula and the historical figure of Vlad the Impaler has spawned a burgeoning tourist industry. Visitors from all over the world come to the country to visit Bran Castle, and the vast forests that surround it. Even though it is not known for sure if Vlad ever stayed there, it has become fixed in the public mind as 'Dracula's Castle', its gothic turrets and remote position serving to underscore its legendary status as the home of the most celebrated literary vampire of all time. Recently, the castle hit the headlines after being returned to its owners, the Van Hapsburg family, 60 years after it was seized by the communists, and has now become one of Romania's top tourist attractions.

Bran Castle, Bran, Romania, Europe

Elizabeth Báthory

The sixteenth-century Hungarian Countess Elizabeth Báthory has gone down in history as the most prolific serial killer of all time, and some believe that she, alongside Vlad the Impaler and others, were inspiration behind Bram Stocker's *Dracula*. Báthory was accused of sexually abusing, torturing, and murdering up to 600 victims at her remote castle, all of them young girls and women, some of them virgins. There were eyewitness accounts of her mutilating the girls' genitals, and biting the flesh off their arms, legs, and faces. Legend has it that she also bathed in her victims' blood, in the belief that it would rejuvenate her, but whether or not this is actually true remains a matter of conjecture. Some historians have also argued that the number of her victims was exaggerated. But whatever the exact details of the case, it is clear that Báthory was a monstrously evil madwoman, whose sadistic treatment of her unfortunate maids went far beyond the callous cruelty towards servants considered acceptable by the nobility at the time.

Madness and incest

Erzsébet Báthory, to give her Hungarian name, was born in 1560 in Nyirbator, Hungary. Her parents were related. Her father, George Báthory came from the Ecsed line of the Báthory family, while her mother, Anna, came from the Somlyo branch. The Báthorys were a powerful Protestant aristocratic family, whose members included princes, warlords, churchmen, and politicians. One of Elizabeth's cousins was the King of Poland, and another went on to become Palatine of Hungary. In order to preserve the purity of their heritage, the Báthory family encouraged intermarriage. This may have contributed to Elizabeth's insanity, which showed itself during her childhood in epileptic fits and uncontrollable rages. Her brother Stephan was also apparently afflicted by mental imbalance, and grew up to be an alcoholic and a notorious sex fiend.

Horrifying punishments

As well as this poor genetic inheritance, the young Elizabeth's sanity may have been affected by witnessing her privileged family's extreme cruelty towards the ordinary people around them. The Hungarian nobility of the time treated their inferiors like animals and worse, and horrific retribution was meted out to anyone who crossed them. In one instance, Elizabeth witnessed the punishment of a gypsy who had been accused of theft. He was sewn into the belly of a horse, with only his head protruding, and left there to die. With such perverse acts of barbarism going on around her, it was hardly surprising that the young Elizabeth came to regard sadistic treatment of her servants as a normal way of life when she grew up.

There were, however, more positive aspects to Elizabeth's experience of childhood. Unlike most other Hungarian aristocrats, some of whom could barely read or write, she received a proper education in Latin and Greek. She was said to have been highly intelligent, and her beauty was also praised.

Unwanted pregnancy

While still a child, she was betrothed to Count Ferenc Nádasdy, a grown man who was renowned as a soldier and athlete. But then, at the age of 14, she became pregnant by one of the peasants on her father's estate. Elizabeth was sent away to live in the countryside and went on to give birth to a daughter. The child was left with a peasant couple and Elizabeth returned to public life.

A year later, Elizabeth married Nádasdy in tremendous style. The Báthorys threw a huge, lavish wedding party with a guest list of 4,500 people. The Holy Roman Emperor himself, Maximilian II, was invited, although he could not attend, citing 'the dangers of travelling in turbulent times' as an excuse. Instead, he sent a large delegation and expensive gifts. The event did much to further the prestige and political power of the Báthory family. What happened subsequently, however, did not.

Satanic rituals

Elizabeth moved with her new husband to the Nádasdy estates around Castle Sárvár. Here the Nádasdys had long held a reputation as cruel overlords, and Ferenc was no exception. He introduced his young wife, still an impressionable teenager, to various cruel ways of punishing their servants, encouraging her to treat them without pity or mercy. There were also rumours that the couple became involved in the occult, calling in black arts practitioners, and performing satanic rituals together.

When Ferenc left home to pursue his studies and his career as a soldier, Elizabeth was left on her own. To while away the time, she travelled between her various castles and took several lovers, even at one stage eloping with one of them, before meekly returning to her husband. She also visited relatives, but in the Báthory-Nádasdy family, this was no respectable round of dull social events. As she soon found out, many of her family members were as sexually voracious as she was. In particular, she struck up a friendship with an aunt who was openly bisexual, and who had many lovers. All this seems to have been tolerated by her husband, and by Hungarian society in general. By all accounts, the Hungarian nobility wielded such power at this period that nobody dared to comment on their decadent way of life, a factor that again encouraged the young Elizabeth to indulge her perversions to the full.

Sadistic wetnurse

Oddly enough, given this hectic sexual activity, Elizabeth found time to bear her husband three daughters and a son. Even more strange, by all accounts she was a kind, affectionate mother, and made sure that her children were well cared for. However, one of her wetnurses, Ilona Jó, later proved to be an accomplice in her crimes, as did several other servants in her entourage. It is yet another contradiction in this bizarre tale that these servants, who were so devoted to the care of young children, should have shown such barbarity in their behaviour towards others.

While her husband was away, Elizabeth took to staying in one of the family's more remote properties, the Cachtice Castle, which had been given to her as a wedding gift from her husband. Here, she used her considerable skills to run the family's business affairs, in some cases providing help and assistance to destitute peasant families. By now her husband was the chief commander of the Hungarian troops,

Count Ferenc Nádasdy (1555-1604)

and was engaged full time in fighting the ongoing war against the Ottomans. Elizabeth was charged with the job of defending the estates against incursions by Ottoman troops; the estates and castles were in strategic positions, including the route to Vienna and the Hungarian border.

Frozen to death

Despite her busy workload, Elizabeth had begun to amuse herself with a pastime that would eventually lead to her downfall: torturing her servant girls. She especially liked to beat them with a barbed lash, or

Postcard depicting Countess Elizabeth Báthory's Castle, Cachtice

cudgel, and then have them dragged naked into the snow. Cold water would then be thrown on them so that they froze to death. She was helped in this gruesome enterprise by three rather sinister figures: Ilona Jó, her wetnurse; a large, imposing local woman called Dorothea Szentes, known as Dorka, who was reputed to be a witch; and a crippled dwarf, Johannes Ujvary, nicknamed Ficzko.

In 1604, Elizabeth's husband Ferenc died, ostensibly from an injury sustained in battle, although there were rumours that he had been attacked by a whore after refusing to pay her for her services. After his death, Elizabeth made Cachtice her permanent home – unfortunately for the

SHE ESPECIALLY LIKED TO BEAT THEM WITH A BARBED LASH

local population, as it turned out. There, she took up with a woman named Anna Darvula, who became her lover. Like Szentes, Darvula was feared as a witch. It later emerged that Darvula was the most sadistic of Báthory's entourage, and that under her tutelage, Báthory became more savage than ever.

Young noblewomen

There was no shortage of young women willing to work at the castle: times were hard for the Hungarian peasantry, and Elizabeth promised high wages for her young female staff. It was only when the maidservants disappeared that rumours began to spread, and the eagerness of the local peasant girls to work for Countess Báthory suddenly abated. Not only this, but at around the same time, in 1609, Elizabeth's lover, Darvula died.

Elizabeth immediately found a new lover, the widow of one of her tenant farmers, Erzsi Majorova, who helped her to solve the problem of how to find victims. At Erzsi's suggestion, the Countess took to inviting the daughters of minor local noblemen to stay at the castle, and meting out the same

e. **Sborenina**

treatment to them. When the girls did not return home, the alarm was raised. Had the Countess continued to torture and murder peasant girls only, her crimes might never have been discovered; it was only when she lost her head and began to prey on the nobility that her reign of terror was discovered.

Family scandal

Under pressure from the fathers of these young women, most of whom were not wealthy but were highly born, the Lord Palatine of Hungary, Count Thurzo, was forced to act. He already knew about the atrocities, having received complaints from a Lutheran minister, Istvan Magyari, but had ignored them, because the Countess was his cousin, and he did not want to have a family scandal on his hands.

Before visiting the scene of the crime, Thurzo consulted with King Matthias of Hungary and Báthory's son and sons-in-law. They agreed that whatever the Countess had done, there should be no public trial. Instead, she would be kept under house arrest and her minions publicly tried in her place.

Walled up

On 30 December 1610, Thurzo went to Cachtice Castle to pay a call on Countess Báthory. There, he and his men found a girl dead in the grounds, and one dying in the hall. Further investigation of the castle dungeons revealed other prisoners awaiting torture. Some were starving, some were very sick, and others were dying. Báthory was arrested, along with four of her accomplices. The Countess was put under house arrest, while the others were taken away for trial.

King Matthias is said to have ordered Báthory's execution at this point, but Thurzo argued that such an act would be bad publicity for the nobility, and so instead, the Countess was walled up in a set of rooms within the castle. Here, she remained for the rest of her days, her only access to the outside world being a small vent for air, and a hatch where food was passed through to her.

Biting flesh

The defendants at the trial included the 'witch' Szentes, the wetnurse Ilona Jó, the dwarf Ujvary, and a washerwoman named Katarina Benicka. Their punishments were every bit as gruesome as their crimes. Szentes and Ilona Jó had their fingernails ripped out with red-hot pincers before being thrown into a firepit, while Ujvary was beheaded and his body burned. Later, Majorova was arrested and executed. Only Benicka escaped death, instead being sentenced to life imprisonment, after witnesses testified that she had only acted under pressure from the others.

During the trial, the true extent of the Countess's sadistic crimes emerged as one witness after another testified against her. In one instance, a 12-year-old girl who had tried to escape from the castle was put into a cage studded with spikes. Ujvary then rolled the cage from side to side and the girl's flesh was torn to shreds. In another episode, the Countess forced several naked girls to lie on the floor of her bedroom, and tortured each of them so cruelly that the other servants had to scoop up the blood using buckets. The Countess later recorded that one of her victims had been so small and weak that, much to her disappointment, she had died quickly.

During the trial, it transpired that Báthory was partial to burning and mutilating her victims' hands, faces, and genitals. She also enjoyed starving them, and watching them freeze to death. Apparently, even when she was ill, she continued her vile perversions. Once, when sick in bed, she commanded Szentes to bring her a maidservant. Szentes did as she was told, holding the girl by the Countess' bedside, whereupon the Countess rose up and bit her, like a dog, sinking her teeth first into her cheek, then into her shoulder, then into her breast.

Bathing in blood?

Estimates regarding the number of Báthory's victims vary greatly. Szentes and Ujvary reported their involvement with 35 young women, other servants with 50 or more. Some servants at Sárvár claimed that between 100 and 200 bodies were taken from the castle. It was claimed that the Countess kept a diary in which she listed over 650 victims. This diary is rumoured to have been kept in Hungarian state archives but – if indeed it exists – it has never been published.

Today, there continue to be many unanswered questions concerning the legend of the 'Blood Countess'. No one knows exactly how many young girls and women met their death at her hands. The rumours about her bathing in the girls' blood have not been confirmed by historical records. In addition, historians remain divided as to the cause of her behaviour. She may have had a genetic inheritance that caused her fits of rage, but this would not account for the extent of her savagery and perversion. Obviously, the mores of the time, in which the nobility treated the peasantry with extreme cruelty, had more than a little influence on her behaviour, as did the fact that her family were extremely rich, powerful and well-connected, so that she was able to pursue her crimes with impunity. But in the end, the reason for her dreadful cruelty, as with so many serial killers, and perversion remains a mystery.

Countess Elizabeth Báthory was found dead in her room on 21 August 1614, lying face down on the floor. A number of plates of food had been left untouched, so it was not clear exactly when her death took place. As one might imagine, there were few, if any, who mourned her passing.

Gilles de Rais was a fifteenth-century nobleman whose lust for blood – in particular, the blood of young boys and girls – marked him out as one of the most prolific serial killers in history. The exact number of his victims is not known, because he burned or buried most of the bodies, but it was believed to have been between 80 and 200. Some estimates have put the figure nearer 600. The details of his crimes, which eventually emerged during his trial, shocked the whole of Europe, and still make disturbing reading today. Like his female counterpart Elizabeth Báthory, who lived a century later, he took advantage of his powerful social position to rape, torture, and murder his innocent victims, and for many years continued his depraved life of criminal violence with impunity.

> **HE TOOK ADVANTAGE OF HIS POWERFUL SOCIAL POSITION TO RAPE, TORTURE, AND MURDER**

The rich heiress

Gilles de Rais was born in 1404, the son of a rich nobleman named Guy de Montmorency-Laval and his wife, Marie de Craon. At the age of nine, his father died. His mother immediately remarried, abandoning Gilles and his brother Rene. Two years later she, too, was dead, and the orphans were sent to live with their grandfather, Jean de Craon. By all accounts, de Craon was an ill-tempered individual who took little interest in his two grandsons other than to try to marry them off, while still children, to various rich heiresses. However, as part of this plan, he also made sure that they received an excellent education. The young Gilles became fluent in Latin, and was said to love music. According to some accounts, he particularly enjoyed reading Suetonius, who described in graphic detail the sexual antics of the debauched Roman emperors. He was also instructed in the chivalric arts of war, and later, went on to distinguish himself greatly in his career as a soldier, fighting beside Joan of Arc.

In his teenage years, Gilles was taken to the court of the French Dauphin, where he impressed the nobility with his intelligence and good looks. De Craon made various unsuccessful attempts to marry him off to some of the richest heiresses in France, including Jeanne de Paynol and Beatrice de Rohan, but to no avail. Eventually, he secured him a betrothal to Catherine Thouars of Brittany, an extremely wealthy heiress of Poitou and La Vendee. The couple were duly married, and Catherine bore him a daughter, Marie, in 1429. By now, Gilles was one of the richest noblemen in France.

Sadistic nature

Early in his career, Gilles de Rais fought for control of Britanny on the side of the Montfort house, against a rival house led by the Count of Penthievre, Olivier De Blois. Eventually, he managed to overcome his enemies and secure the release of the Duke of Montfort. For this, he was rewarded with land grants, which the Breton government of the day converted into monetary gifts for him. In between his fighting engagements, he spent time at court, learning the refined manners of the day, and enjoying the company of the Dauphin, all of which helped to further his career. From 1427 to 1435, he served as a commander in the French royal army, gaining a reputation as a courageous fighter on the battlefield, in combat at Saint Lo and Le Mans. In one instance, during a battle for the control of the Chateau of Lude, he climbed a tower and killed the captain of the opposing side.

However, it was during these battles that de Rais' sadistic nature began to show itself. He appeared to positively revel in the carnage, and took a personal delight in killing his enemies, whether running them through with a sword or trampling on them with his horse. At the time, this was not generally frowned upon; indeed, the reverse was true, and instead of being reviled as a brutal sadist, Gilles was held up as an example of a brave, upstanding young knight.

Joan of Arc

In 1429, Gilles de Rais encountered the infamous Joan of Arc. Joan, a 17-year-old peasant girl, had come before the Dauphin, telling him that she knew it to be her destiny to defeat the English army, who at the time were laying siege to the city of Orleans. The Dauphin thought that she was out of her mind, but decided anyway to send her to Orleans with Gilles, who was fascinated by the peasant girl's bravery – and her mannish looks. Much to the Dauphin's amazement, Joan went on to defeat the English, with Gilles at her side.

Exactly how important the young knight's presence was remains a matter of some historical controversy, but there is no doubt that his early association with the Maid of Orleans brought him tremendous fame and honour. (However, when Joan of Arc was burned at the stake only a few years later, Gilles made sure to play down this association.) He was duly appointed Marshal of France, and rewarded with further riches. After a few more years of fighting, he retired to his estates, indulging his taste for luxury by mounting expensive religious services and acquiring an extensive library.

HE APPEARED TO POSITIVELY REVEL IN THE CARNAGE

Secret vices

Retirement from the army, and from the opportunity to kill and maim on the battlefield, seems to have had a dreadful effect on the rich young knight. He began to spend his fortune recklessly, producing a theatrical spectacle called 'The Mystery of the Siege of Orleans' in which he played the leading role. The production employed hundreds of actors and costumes, and the audience was treated to sumptuous food and drink. Not surprisingly, he soon began to run out of money, and had to sell much of his property. His brother Rene was so worried about Gilles' spendthrift ways that he asked the King to help. The King issued an edict forbidding him to sell any more land. His hands tied, Gilles turned his attentions elsewhere.

Gilles de Rais (1404-40) performs sorcery on his victims

Gilles de Rais was accused of evoking the Devil by sacrificing small children. For this and other wickedness he was condemned to death.

Torture and murder

It was around this time that de Rais began to indulge his secret vices. He procured a young street boy named Poitou, brought him to his chateau and raped him. He was then about to cut his throat, when a companion pointed out to him that the boy might make a good page. Gilles spared him, and Poitou became one of his minions. Others were not so lucky.

STRIPPED, HUNG UP BY A HOOK, AND TORTURED

In the years that followed, Gilles de Rais went on to torture and murder a succession of children, aged between six and 16, most of them boys. According to witnesses, he preferred to commit his vile crimes with boys, but would use girls if necessary. The craving for blood would come upon him like an epileptic fit, as if he were a vampire, and he would not rest until his thirst had been quenched.

He would send out a servant to lure a boy to his chateau. De Rais would pretend to treat him kindly, petting him and offering him drink. He would then be stripped, hung up by a hook, and tortured. Then one of his minions would cut the boy's throat, which apparently gave de Rais immense delight. After this, the body would be disembowelled and de Rais would play with it, squatting in the entrails and masturbating. Once he had had his fill, he would faint and be carried to bed, to rest while his servants disposed of the body. They did this by dismembering and burning it. In some cases, two boys would be procured at once, and one forced to watch the torture and murder of the other, before his own time came.

It is hard to believe that such crimes went unpunished for years, but tragically, that is what occurred. Most of de Rais' victims were young boys of low standing, and since he himself was a nobleman, his actions were not questioned, as was the norm during this period of European history.

Demons and snakes

As well as his bloodlust, de Rais also had a fascination for the occult. He was, by now, running short of money, so he turned to the forbidden art of alchemy as a source. He found a magician named Fontanelle, who claimed to have conjured up a demon called Barron. De Rais agreed to sell his soul to this demon in exchange for the power to make gold. So Fontanelle, de Rais, and his cousin de Sille, entered the dungeon of one of his castles at night to perform the magic rites. However, all that happened was that the roof fell in, and de Rais narrowly escaped with his life.

Not deterred, de Rais hired another magician, a handsome young man called Francois Prelati, to continue his search for gold. Prelati advised him that a child's blood and body parts would have to be offered

to the Devil, and performed various rites that appealed to the gullible de Rais, but failed to yield the treasure he sought. On one occasion, Prelati pretended to have sustained a severe beating from the Devil; on another, he told his employer that a huge pile of gold was waiting for him in the next room, but that it was guarded by a large green snake. De Rais beat a hasty retreat, only to find when he returned that the gold had mysteriously vanished.

Madness and depravity

Not surprisingly, during these years of madness and depravity, de Rais' family shunned him, but when they heard that he was about to sell one of his castles, the Chateau Champtoce, in defiance of the royal edict, they seized it. De Rais feared that they would find many bodies of murdered children there, but fortunately for him, they did not. However, as a precaution, he began to remove bodies from his other castles, and later took the opportunity to cover his traces at Champtoce.

By now, his behaviour was becoming ever more erratic. He sold the Chateau Mer Morte, but then decided to take it back, stealing the keys from the new owner's brother, Jean de Ferron, who happened to be a priest. De Rais and his men turned up at the church, dragged the priest away, and beat him until he offered up the keys. Afterwards, de Rais stayed the night in a town called Vannes, where to celebrate, he raped and decapitated a 10-year-old boy, afterwards throwing the child's body into a latrine.

'Vices against nature'

This attack on the priest was the chance that the authorities had been waiting for. De Rais was arrested and in 1440, was summoned before the court. A large number of witnesses, including the parents of some of the children, gave testimony against him. According to the bizarre morality of the day, the main charge against him was heresy (because he had entered the church violently and attacked the priest) but he was also accused of other offences, including the rape and murder of the children. In total, he faced 47 charges that ranged from 'the abuse of clerical privilege' to 'the conjuration of demons', and 'vices against nature'.

In all, there were 110 witnesses at the trial, which attracted tremendous attention throughout France. History records that the servants' descriptions of the murders were so horrifying that the judges ordered parts of their testimony to be deleted. One of de Rais' servants, Etienne Corillait, known as Poitou – who had personal experience of de Rais' sadism, having been procured as a murder victim himself, and then spared – gave a graphic account of the way de Rais went about extracting maximum enjoyment from his hideous crimes: 'He had considerable pleasure in watching the heads of children separated from their bodies. Sometimes he made an incision behind the neck to make them die slowly, at which he became very excited ... sometimes he would ask, when they were dead, which of them had the most beautiful head.'

Corillait also described, in graphic detail, how de Rais masturbated over the children's bodies, both when they were dead and when they were alive.

> ## HE HAD CONSIDERABLE PLEASURE IN WATCHING THE HEADS OF CHILDREN SEPARATED FROM THEIR BODIES

Final execution

Some believe that these accounts, extracted as they were under torture, were exaggerated. Certainly, de Rais himself was so brutally tortured that by the end of the trial, he was confessing to anything. His trial was farcical, even by the standards of the day, and the main objection to his behaviour seemed to be that it was heretical, rather than the fact that he had murdered dozens, if not hundreds, of innocent children. Eventually, he was sentenced to death, garrotted and his body thrown onto a funeral pyre. However, before the pyre was lit, his family were allowed to take the body away for burial.

In his chronicles of the period, the French nobleman Enguerrand de Monstrelet, wrote: 'The greater part of the nobles of Brittany, more especially his own kindred, were in utmost grief and confusion at his disgraceful death. Before this event, he was much renowned as a most valiant knight at arms.'

The legacy of de Rais

Today, the extent of de Rais' crimes is the subject of some controversy among historians. There is no doubt that his trial was carried out with such disregard for the law that the findings of it cannot be seen as entirely valid. De Rais was not allowed to give testimony in his defence, and nor were any of his family, friends, or servants. Indeed, the ecclesiastic and secular authorities showed such bias in their attitude towards him that it is hard not to doubt the accuracy of their conclusions.

In her book, *The Witch Cult of Western Europe*, anthropologist Margaret Murray argues that de Rais was possibly involved in a fertility cult centred around the pagan goddess Diana, and that he was tried and executed, like Joan of Arc before him, for heresy. Others have suggested that de Rais might have been framed by the Church, or by other elements within the French nobility, as part of a plot to take over his remaining lands. It is certainly true that his crazed behaviour made him an easy target for any power group wishing to divest him of his rapidly dwindling estates.

However, the testimony of so many witnesses, including his young victims' parents, would suggest that Gilles was indeed guilty of serial murder, and that after his glorious days as a young soldier, he descended into a nightmare world of madness, debauchery, and violence that only ended when he was finally put to death, on 26 October 1440.

The chateau at Champtoce-sur-Loire, one of the Bluebeard Castles, which belonged to Gilles de Rais

Peter Kürten

The Vampire of Düsseldorf was perhaps the most notorious among the spate of serial killers who terrorized Germany in the years between the world wars. This was a time of terrible poverty in the country, and in the resulting social breakdown, crime of all kinds, including the murder, abduction, and abuse of both adults and children, was rife. At the peak of Peter Kürten's activities during 1929 he carried out so many attacks against such a wide variety of victims that the police assumed there must be several murderers at large, not just one. Kürten was nicknamed 'the Vampire' because of his obsession with his victims' blood. He was believed to drink it, but there is no firm evidence that this was the case. What is indisputable is that he was a sadist who derived pleasure from killing, in particular watching his victims' blood drain away from their bodies.

Child murderer

Peter Kürten was born into desperate poverty in Köln-Mullheim on 26 May 1883. He was one of a family of thirteen who all lived in one room. His father was a violent drunk who would regularly come home and rape his wife in front of the rest of the family. Later, this vicious and violent man's attentions turned to his 13-year-old daughter. It was only at this point that his wife put her foot down and had him arrested. Kürten senior was sent to prison for raping his daughter. While he was in prison, his wife divorced him.

Sadly, however, this appalling start to his life had a marked effect on the young Peter. As a child, he became friendly with a dogcatcher who lived in the same building. The dogcatcher was a sadist who tortured and sexually assaulted animals and taught Peter to do likewise. At the same time, Peter started to sexually abuse his sisters, as he had seen his father do.

By his own account, Kürten carried out his first murders aged nine, when he contrived to drown two of his friends while playing on a raft in the Rhine. However, this was taken to be an accident, and he was not charged with the murders. If he had been, many people's lives might have been saved as a result.

Sadist on the loose

With the arrival of puberty, things went from bad to worse. Kürten became a compulsive masturbator who started to experiment with bestiality. During intercourse with sheep, he took to stabbing the animals, which he found he particularly enjoyed.

By the age of 16, he had run away from home. He supported himself by petty crime, which in turn led to regular short spells in prison. When not in prison he tended to strike up relationships with masochistic prostitutes considerably older than himself. During this period he also claimed to have carried out his first murder as an adult, strangling a girl during sex some time in 1899. No body was ever found so this claim cannot be verified. A year later, however, he was jailed for two years for attempting to shoot a girl and a further two for theft.

On release in 1904, Kürten was drafted into the army. He soon deserted and struck up a new interest, setting fire to barns and haystacks in the hope of burning a tramp

A dummy dressed in the clothes of one of Kürten's victims, which was taken by the police round the dance-halls and cabarets of Düsseldorf.

alive. The following year, he received his longest prison sentence yet, seven years for theft.

While in prison he claims to have poisoned several inmates, though once again, this proved to be unverifiable. What is clear is that his extended stay in prison clearly stoked his violent sexual fantasies to fever pitch.

On release in 1912, Kürten raped a servant girl. A year later, he broke into an inn and found a young girl asleep in bed. He strangled her and then cut her throat, revelling in the sight of the blood spurting out of her neck. Despite leaving a handkerchief with his initials embroidered on the scene, he got away with the crime and the girl's uncle was blamed. He had recently had a bitter row with her father and therefore was suspected of carrying out the murder.

A changed man?

Kürten went on to attack several more women, none of them fatally, before once again being sent to jail, this time for eight years. Released in 1921, Kürten moved to the town of Altenburg and for a while seemed to be a changed man. He met a local woman and married her, settled down to a steady job as a moulder in a factory, and became an active trade unionist. However, when in 1925 the couple moved to Düsseldorf, his self-control began to slip. Perhaps it was the fact that he had previously committed so many crimes there; perhaps his marriage was beginning to fail; perhaps he became tired of his respectable life. Whatever the reason, he went on back to his old ways. Over the next four years he would carry out several sexual assaults on women, generally involving attempts at strangulation. Then, in February 1929, his reign of terror began in earnest.

Brutal murders

On 3 February, Kürten ran up to a complete stranger, a woman named Frau Kuhn, in the street. He proceeded to stab her 24 times, including several blows to the temple, and then ran away, leaving her lying on the pavement. Remarkably, she survived. His next victim was not so lucky. On 9 February, only six days later, Kürten attacked a nine-year-old girl named Rose Ohliger. He stabbed her 13 times, once again including blows to the temple, which were sufficient to kill her. Semen was found on her body, it was thought that he may have inserted it into her vagina after death, with his finger. He then attempted to burn the child's corpse and left the partially burnt body on a building site.

Five day later he killed again. This time his victim was a man, a 45-year-old mechanic by the name of Scheer. He stabbed Scheer 20 times, once again including wounds to the temple. The police were baffled. The stab wounds on the victim's body indicated that this was the same murderer as before, but in terms of the victim, there seemed to be no pattern at all. Whoever it was who was doing the killings seemed to strike at random, without any obvious sexual or other motivation.

Random killings

Whatever demons that drove Kürten were satisfied for a while. He bided his time while a drifter was arrested and briefly suspected of being the killer. When the drifter was cleared, Kürten waited until August then struck again. Three more victims were attacked in apparently random stabbings but survived. Then on 24 August, two children, ten-year-old Gertrude Hamacher and 14-year-old Louise Lenzen, were accosted

French actress Marie-France Pisier together with actor, director, and screenwriter
Robert Hossein on the set of Hossein's movie *Le Vampire de Düsseldorf*

as they walked home from a fair. Kürten came out of the shadows and strangled them before cutting Gertrude's throat and decapitating Louise.

The next day he accosted another woman, Gertrude Schelkter, near a different fair. When he asked her for sex, she replied that she would rather die, to which he responded, 'Well, die then'. He went on to stab her several times. Surprisingly, she survived the attack, and was able to give the police a description of her assailant.

Panic response

Three more attempted strangulations followed in September of that year before Kürten once more confused the police by switching weapon. His next two victims, Ida Reuter and Elizabeth Dirries, both had their heads bashed in by blows from a hammer. Kürten then returned to a previous modus operandi for his next victim, five-year-old Gertrude Albernaman. Kürten strangled and stabbed her 36 times. By now, it appeared that Kürten was crying out to be caught. He sent directions as to where her body could be found to a local newspaper. He followed that stunt up by informing the paper of the whereabouts of a previously unknown victim, Maria Hahn, whom he had stabbed and raped back in August. By now, residents of the area were becoming panic-stricken by the murders, and not only Germany but the whole world was nervously waiting for the monster's next move. Not since Jack the Ripper had a community been so traumatized by a single maniac.

Final capture

Kürten responded by going quiet once again. For a while it seemed as if he had simply disappeared. But on 14 May 1930, he picked up a young woman named Mari Budlick who was looking for work. He took her to his house, then took her to the woods, where he attempted to rape her. She resisted and amazingly, he simply let her go. She went to the police and told them where her would-be rapist lived. Even then, Kürten initially evaded capture. When he saw the police arrive at his house, he quickly left and rented a room round the corner. Then he summoned his wife and confessed to her. His concern was that she should receive the reward money for turning him in. She agreed to the plan and on 24 May, arranged for his handover to the police. When they approached him, he simply smiled and said, 'There is no need to be afraid'.

Kürten, it seemed, was as relieved as anyone else that it was over, he was quickly tried, convicted of nine murders, and sentenced to death by beheading. In prison waiting for execution he was extensively interviewed by psychiatrists. He told them that he was looking forward to his death – he could imagine no greater thrill than hearing the blood spurt out from his severed neck.

The sentence was carried out on 2 July 1931. Today, Kürten is remembered as the 'Vampire of Düsseldorf', one of the most bloodthirsty serial killers of all time.

Fritz Haarmann

In the early years of the twentieth century, the term 'serial killer' had not been coined. Instead, media pundits used a variety of terms from European folklore to describe killers who struck again and again, seemingly at random. What we would now call a serial killer would be described, especially in Northern Europe, as a vampire, a werewolf, or a 'wolf man'.

Thus it was that Fritz Haarmann, a murderer who committed a series of shocking crimes in the period after World War I, was dubbed 'the Vampire of Hanover'. In actual fact, most of the murders he committed involved beheading his victims, knifing them, and cutting up their bodies, which he then – horrifyingly – sold as pork meat on the black market. It was only towards the end of his grisly run of murders that Haarmann began to bite his victims in the neck, sucking out their blood. Nevertheless, he went down in history as a real-life vampire, and his chilling legacy of violence and murder is still part of the city's heritage today. Haarmann is also thought to be the first serial killer whose case was widely reported in the press, causing a media frenzy that culminated in a sensational trial, and giving him the dubious honour of being forever remembered as 'The Vampire of Hanover'.

Savage onslaught

Fritz Haarmann was one of the first serial killers to hit the headlines in modern times, having confessed to the murders of at least 27 young men and boys in the town of Hanover between 1918 and 1924. What made Haarmann uniquely terrifying was the bizarre mixture of frenzy and orderliness that characterized his crimes. He would kill his victims in a savage onslaught, biting through their windpipes as he raped them. Then with considerable care he would remove their clothes and sell them, dismember the bodies, dispose of the bones, cook the flesh, and finally sell it on the black market as pork.

If this seems hard to believe, one should remember that Germany in the years after World War I was on the brink of starvation. People were so hungry that few questions were asked as to the provenance of food, especially meat. In addition, the basic structures of government, law and order, and social services had almost entirely broken down, so that the disappearance of individuals – especially those who were not from the more wealthy classes – was not often remarked upon. Life was cheap, and horrific murderers like Haarmann flourished in such circumstances.

Epileptic fits

Fritz (Friedrich) Haarmann was born on 25 October, 1879, in Hanover. He was the sixth child of Ollie and Johanna. Ollie was a locomotive stoker, a drunk and a womanizer. Johanna was older than him, 41 at the time Fritz was born and in poor health. Fritz, the baby of the family, was his mother's particular favourite and he often sided with her against his father. As a child he preferred dolls to boys' toys. More worrying at the time was a fondness for frightening people, particularly his sisters. He liked to play games that involved tying them up or scaring them by tapping on their windows at night.

Haarmann's mother died when he was 12 and his feuding with his father intensified. After school he tried an apprenticeship as a locksmith. When that failed, he was sent to military school. After six months there, however, he was sent home because he seemed to be suffering from epileptic fits.

Child molester

Back in Hanover, the young Haarmann took to molesting children. Complaints were made and he was examined by a doctor, who sent him to the insane asylum. This turned out to be a deeply traumatizing experience. Haarmann eventually escaped and fled to Switzerland before returning to Hanover at the turn of the twentieth century. To all appearances, he seemed to be a reformed character. He married a woman named Erna Loewert and seemed ready to settle down. This peaceful interlude was not to last, when his wife became pregnant, Haarmann left her and joined the army.

After his discharge in 1903, Haarmann returned to Hanover once again and became involved in petty crime. He was arrested for burglary, pick pocketing, and small-scale cons. In 1914 he was convicted for a warehouse burglary and sent to prison, enabling him to escape combat as a soldier in World War I. On his release from prison in 1918, he stepped into a Germany that was traumatized by war, and whose people were suffering intense poverty and the breakdown of ordered society. Crime was flourishing as people struggled to make ends meet. This was the ideal environment for a man like Haarmann. He immediately joined a smuggling ring and simultaneously became a police informer, managing to profit from both sides at once.

Preying on the homeless

Another feature of the post-war years was the number of homeless and displaced people milling around the city. Many of the younger ones resorted to prostitution and thus, it became easy for Haarmann to pick up young boys. In particular he liked to frequent the railway station and find likely prospects there. Often he would introduce himself as Detective Haarmann and use that pretext to get the boys to go with him. And where once he had been satisfied with simple sexual abuse, now he needed to kill his victims to fully satisfy his lust.

One of his first victims was named Friedel Rothe. Rothe's parents found out that their son had gone with 'Detective Haarmann' and the police went round to Haarmaan's apartment but failed to notice the boy's severed head hidden behind the stove. Shortly afterwards Haarmann received a nine month prison sentence for indecency. On his release he met a young homosexual called Hans Grans. They entered into a sexual relationship and moved in together, next they became business partners, trading on the black market with Fritz continuing to also act as a police informer. Over the next couple of years their business began to include a gruesome new sideline: selling the clothes and the cooked flesh of Haarmann's victims.

Meat inspection

For the most part their victims were not missed. Even when they were, the authorities seemed to make elementary blunders in following up clues: the parents of one victim told the police they suspected Grans of having been the murderer. Grans was temporarily in prison at the time of the accusation, but Haarmann was never

Fritz Haarmann and the son of his landlady with the jacket that helped prove Haarmann's guilt.

investigated, even though he visited the house of the parents pretending to be a criminologist and laughing hysterically as they told him of their fears.

On another occasion, a suspicious customer took some of Haarmann's meat to the authorities for examination, the police expert, without making any tests, duly pronounced it to be pork. Thus, it seemed to be the case that as long as the murders were confined to a homosexual netherworld, the authorities preferred to turn a blind eye.

MORE HUMAN SKULLS WERE FOUND

Fritz Haarmann sentenced to death for killing 27 young men, is shown here, heavily guarded, as he walks from jail to the court house for the trial

Human skulls

All that changed in May 1924 when, first one, and then, over the next few weeks, several more, human skulls were found by the river Leine. The authorities tried to damp down the public's fear, suggesting that it was all a macabre joke, the skulls having been left there by graverobbers. However when, on 24 July, children playing in the area found a sack full of human bones, there

was no stopping the panic. In all, the police found 500 bones belonging to at least 27 different bodies.

The police investigated all the local sex offenders, amongst them Fritz Haarmann, but still found no evidence to connect him to the apparent murders. In the end it was Haarmann's own over-confidence that led to his downfall. For some reason – conceivably to try and stop himself form committing another murder – he took a 15-year-old boy to the police to report the boy for insolent behaviour. Once under arrest the boy accused Haarmann of making sexual advances. Haarmann was then arrested and his flat was searched. The police found garments belonging to some of the missing children, some of them bloodstained. Haarmann explained them away saying he was a dealer in used clothing and he had no idea where they had come from.

Death by decapitation

However, after a week in custody under heavy questioning, Haarmann finally confessed to the murders. He took the detectives to a number of sites around Hanover where he had buried further bodies. He seemed to take macabre pride in his crimes. His testimony only varied when it came to the role of Hans Grans, whom he alternately blamed and exculpated.

When it came to trial Haarmann was sentenced to death while the jury decided that Grans was no more than an accessory. He was sentenced to 12 years in prison. Haarmann appeared to thoroughly enjoy his trial, conducting his own defence, smoking cigars and complaining about the presence of women in the courtroom. It was his final act of bravado, however. On 15 April 1925 he was, like many of his victims before him, decapitated.

CHAPTER 5

Vampires of the Imagination

In 1797 the famous German writer and polymath Johann Wolfgang von Goethe wrote *The Bride of Corinth*: A young woman returns from the dead as a vampire to her parents' house and seduces a young man who is staying with them. Her parents, desperate to see her again, interrupt the pair as they are making love, whereupon the young woman explains that she has been allowed back from the underworld to taste a night of passion with a man, but now that they have broken the spell, she must return again. She then becomes a corpse once more, before their very eyes.

That same year, 1797, the well-known English poet Samuel Taylor Coleridge began the first part of a long narrative poem, *Christabel*. In the poem, the central character, Christabel, meets a mysterious woman, Geraldine, who appears to have magical powers. Although she is very beautiful, and makes a close and trusting friend of the innocent Christabel, as well as Christabel's father, she later reveals an underlying demonic quality. Although vampires are never mentioned in Coleridge's poem, the setting and emotional dynamic between the characters, especially between Christabel and Geraldine, have all the characteristic features of a vampire story.

Coleridge's friend Robert Southey, another of the Romantic poets, as they were known, also penned a ballad concerning a vampire, *The Old Woman of Berkeley*. In this story, a seemingly respectable old woman, among whose children are a monk and a nun, summons her offspring to her side before she dies. To their surprise, she reveals that she has lived a life of terrible sin, and asks them to bolt and chain her coffin so that the devil cannot come for her. She explains:

> *'All kind of sin have I rioted in,*
> *And the judgement now must be,*
> *But I secured my children's souls,*
> *Oh! pray, my children, for me!*
>
> *'I have 'nointed myself with infant's fat,*
> *The fiends have been my slaves,*
> *From sleeping babes I have suck'd the breath,*
> *And breaking by charms the sleep of death,*
> *I have call'd the dead from their graves.*
>
> *'And the Devil will fetch me now in fire,*
> *My witchcrafts to atone;*
> *And I who have troubled the dead man's grave*
> *Shall never have rest in my own.*

The children do their best for their mother, but their efforts to spare her from the Devil are in vain, and he duly arrives in a mighty blast of fire and wind, to take her off to hell.

CHRISTABEL.

PART THE FIRST.

T

IS

THE MIDDLE OF NIGHT BY THE
CASTLE CLOCK,
AND THE OWLS HAVE AWAK-
ENED THE CROWING COCK,
TU—WHIT!——TU—WHOO!
AND HARK, AGAIN! THE CROW-
ING COCK,
HOW DROWSILY IT CREW.

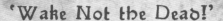

'Wake Not the Dead!'

At the height of the Gothic craze for ghost stories and tales of the supernatural, a Northern English poet called John Stagg, known as the Blind Bard of Cumberland, wrote a poem called *The Vampire*. In the preface, he explained that the story was:

founded on an opinion or report which prevailed in Hungary, and several parts of Germany, towards the beginning of the last century. It was then asserted, that, in several places, dead persons had been known to leave their graves, and, by night, to revisit the habitations of their friends whom, by suckosity, they drained of their blood as they slept. The person thus phlebotomized was sure to become a Vampyre in their turn; and if it had not been for a lucky thought of the clergy, who ingeniously recommended staking them in their graves, we should by this time have had a greater swarm of blood-suckers than we have at present, numerous as they are.

SHE FEASTS ON THE BLOOD UNTIL ALL ARE DEAD

Another Romantic poet to write about vampires was Johann Ludwig von Tiecke, in his poem, *The Bride of the Grave*, and in his story, *Wake Not the Dead!*. The story was part of a collection of folk tales on the model of the Brothers Grimm, and was published in English in 1823. It tells of Walter, a lord, and his wife, Brunhilda. Although they share a passionate erotic love, Brunhilda has a dreadful temper, and terrorizes the household. When Brunhilda dies suddenly, Walter takes a new wife, Swanhilda and they have two children. But

Walter begins to miss his lustful nights with Brunhilda, and compels a sorcerer to wake her from the dead by giving her corpse blood to drink. Brunhilda returns to life, more beautiful than ever, but with a worse temper, and a pair of razor-sharp fangs to boot. She feasts on the blood of the household staff and the family until all are dead. Finally, she turns on Walter himself. Walter kills her, and then takes another woman, but while in his new love's embrace, she turns into a snake. The castle catches fire, the walls fall in, and as he is crushed to death, he hears a voice command, 'Wake Not the Dead!'.

'Mad, bad, and dangerous to know'

The theme of the seductive enchantress as harbinger of death was a very popular one among the Romantic poets, including John Keats, whose poems *Lamia* and *La Belle Dame Sans Merci* both evoke the idea of a fabulously beautiful woman who turns out to be a supernatural being. In these stories, the woman typically charms a mortal man into spiritual slavery, leaving his life in ruins.

Lord Byron, one of the leading Romantic poets, famously described by his married lover Lady Caroline Lamb as 'mad, bad, and dangerous to know', also reprised this theme in his poem, *The Giaour*, which actually mentions vampires by name. The story concerns a Turkish girl, Leila, who falls in love with an infidel ('the giaour' of the title). The infidel kills Leila's husband, and is punished by becoming a vampire. It is thought that Lord Byron first heard of vampires on his 'grand tour' of Europe at the turn of the nineteenth century.

Tales of the Dead

Lord Byron also served as a model for the first real vampire story, John William Polidori's *The Vampyre*, published in 1819. Polidori was Byron's personal physician, and in the summer of 1816, he stayed with Byron in Switzerland at the Villa Diodati beside Lake Geneva. There, he and Byron spent time with Byron's friends Percy Shelley, Shelley's fiancé Mary Godwin, and Mary's stepsister, Claire Clairmont. Claire had had an affair with Byron in London, and was pregnant with his child, but Byron refused to be in her company unless Shelley and her sister were present.

The little circle of friends were kept indoors for several days that summer as it rained incessantly. To while away the time, they read tales from *Fantasmagoriana*, a collection of horror fiction later translated into English as *Tales of the Dead*. They then proposed a 'ghost writing' contest, and took to writing their own stories. Mary Godwin, who later became Mary Shelley, came up with the idea for her novel *Frankenstein*, perhaps the most famous horror story of all time.

Lord Byron, for his part, began a story concerning a narrator who embarks on a 'grand tour' with an old man, Augustus Darvell. As the journey progresses, Darvell becomes weaker and weaker, until, when they reach a cemetery, his face turns black and his body begins to decompose. Byron had intended to have Darvell come to life again as a vampire, but never finished the story, and it was left to his friend Polidori to revive it.

The debauched aristocrat

Not long after this sojourn in Switzerland, John Polidori and Lord Byron fell out, and Polidori went travelling, eventually

returning to London. However, Polidori had been inspired by Lord Byron's fragment to write a short story of his own, *The Vampyre*. Its hero, Lord Ruthven, a bored and spoiled aristocrat, was based on the personality of Lord Byron himself. 'Lord Ruthven' was a name originally used in Lady Caroline Lamb's novel *Glenarvon*, a thinly disguised portrait of her former lover.

Polidori's story was published in the *New Monthly Magazine* as 'A Tale by Lord Byron' in 1819. Both Polidori and Byron protested that Byron was not the author, but to no avail. At this period, Lord Byron was so famous that the public – particularly his armies of female admirers – were clamouring for his work. Byron had not only made a name for himself as a writer, but his outrageous behaviour had scandalized English society, and he had been forced to leave the country, accused of incest and sodomy. Yet although he was reviled in many quarters, like many of today's celebrities, his bad behaviour and many shocking sexual liaisons only made him more attractive to his female fans.

The story became an immediate sensation, partly because Byron was believed to have written it, but also because it met the public's growing enthusiasm for gothic horror stories. Moreover, it was highly original, since it transformed the ugly, brutish vampire of Slavic folklore into the suave, charismatic, upper-class villain that we are so familiar with today.

The Victorian Vampire Craze

As mentioned earlier, the idea of the revenant, a spirit returning from the dead to visit a family member or lover, is a very ancient one that crosses many cultures, and was a strong theme in much European folklore. In the nineteenth century, this theme found its way into English literature, not just in poems, but in stories as well. The first of these stories was written by a woman, Elizabeth Grey, whose ghostly tale *The Skeleton Count*, or *The Vampire Mistress* was published in 1828 in the weekly paper *The Casket*. Grey was a well-known and very prolific popular novelist of the period. Most of her work remains obscure today, but this story was to assure her a place in literary history.

Varney the Vampire

Many of Grey's stories appeared in the so-called 'penny dreadfuls', serial stories that appeared in cheap editions over a period of weeks. Each of the editions cost a penny, and was printed on pulp paper, usually with a lurid illustration on the front to match the contents. The 'penny dreadfuls' were bought, much as comics used to be, mainly by children, teenagers and young adults. One of the most popular of all these series was a story called *Varney the Vampire*, or *The Feast of Blood* by James Malcolm Rymer. (Some attribute the series to another gothic horror writer, Thomas Preskett Prest, creator of another famous character in the horror genre, Sweeney Todd.) So popular was Varney that in 1847, the series was published in book form, in a mammoth edition running to over 800 pages, with 220 chapters, and illustrated by an unknown artist who nevertheless vividly captured the horrific exploits of this gruesome hero.

The series featured a vampire, Sir Francis Varney, and his attacks on a family called the Bannerworths. Varney's motivation for troubling the Bannerworths was never entirely clear; nor was the cause of his death, or the circumstances of his revival, allowing the author to engage in various speculative tales about how his corpse was reanimated. As the stories progress, we find out that Varney has been cursed with vampirism after betraying a royalist to Oliver Cromwell and accidentally killing his son in a fit of rage, and over the course of the series, Varney becomes a more and more sympathetic character: at the end, desperately unhappy about his condition, he finally throws himself into a volcano, and disappears into the fiery depths for ever.

The 'sympathetic' vampire

Varney introduced several important features to vampire stories, and some of these have become staples of horror fiction up to the present day. He has supernatural powers, is able to hypnotize people, and has prominent fangs, which, when he feeds off a victim's blood, leave two puncture marks on the skin. He does not fear garlic

No. 1.] Nos. 2, 3 and 4 are Presented, Gratis, with this No. [Price 1d.

VARNEY THE VAMPIRE.

OR THE

FEAST OF BLOOD

A ROMANCE OF EXCITING INTEREST.

BY THE AUTHOR OF
"GRACE RIVERS; OR, THE MERCHANT'S DAUGHTER."

LONDON: E. LLOYD, SALISBURY-SQUARE, AND ALL BOOKSELLERS.

Cover of the first edition of *Varney the Vampire*, published in London in 1853.

THE FEAST OF BLOOD.

Vampire hunters from *Varney the Vampire*

or crosses, can withstand daylight, and is able to act as an ordinary human being – for example, he can eat normal food and drink, although it does not give him sustenance. It is only when he is hungry that he exhibits the characteristics of a vampire. Most significant of all, we are able to feel sympathy for him as an individual suffering from a horrible condition; through the story of the mythical vampire, we come to empathize with the feelings of an outsider, forever doomed as an outcast from human society because of a past sin, or because of his nature, or both. In this sense, Varney is a precursor of the contemporary 'sympathetic' vampire, which today excites so much interest in romantic horror fiction.

Carmilla: the lesbian vampire?

The next milestone in the history of vampire fiction was a gothic novella entitled *Carmilla*, which was published in 1872 in the magazine *The Dark Blue*. The author was Joseph Sheridan Le Fanu, a famous writer of ghost stories, who came from a well-known literary family that included a number of playwrights and novelists. Two illustrators were employed to work on his book, resulting in some confusion as to the appearance of certain characters, but in essence, the story concerns an innocent young woman, Laura, and her close friend, Carmilla, who turns out to be a vampire.

In true gothic style, the story begins with a remote castle in a forest in Austria, where a young woman, Laura, and her widowed father live in solitary splendour. Laura tells of a dream she had as a young girl in which a beautiful stranger came to her room and bit her on the chest. As a teenager, she longs for a companion, and is disappointed when her father receives a message to say that the young lady he has sent for, Bertha

Rheinfeldt, has died suddenly. However, by chance, a carriage accident takes place outside the castle, and a young woman, Carmilla, emerges from it, injured. Laura and Carmilla immediately recognize each other from the dream they had as children. Meanwhile, Carmilla's mother explains to Laura's father that she must journey on, and it is decided that Carmilla will be left at the castle.

Gloating eyes and hot lips

In the weeks that follow, Carmilla and Laura become close friends, but Carmilla refuses to divulge anything about her family or former life. Carmilla also has other peculiarities. Her moods change abruptly, from extreme sweetness to intense anger; she sleeps a great deal during the day, and is often found sleepwalking at night. In addition, she hates the sound of Christian hymns. Most disturbingly, she begins to show a romantic attachment to Laura, which Laura finds repugnant:

Sometimes after an hour of apathy, my strange and beautiful companion would take my hand and hold it with a fond pressure, renewed again and again; blushing softly, gazing in my face with languid and burning eyes, and breathing so fast that her dress rose and fell with the tumultuous respiration. It was like the ardour of a lover; it embarrassed me; it was hateful and yet overpowering; and with gloating eyes she drew me to her, and her hot lips travelled along my cheek in kisses; and she would whisper, almost in sobs, "You are mine, you shall be mine, and you and I are one for ever."

Destroying the vampire

As a result of this unwanted attention, Laura begins to become anxious, and experiences severe nightmares in which she dreams of a cat-like animal that attacks her, biting her chest, and then turns into a beautiful young woman.

We then find out what happened to the unfortunate Bertha. According to her guardian, Bertha was attacked by a young lady called Millarca, who came to the house in exactly the same circumstances as Carmilla. The guardian recounts how, on realizing Millarca was a vampire, he lay in wait for her, and saw her enter the room as a cat-like creature. The creature bit Bertha on the neck and then left, taking her human form once more. Shortly afterwards, Bertha died.

It then transpires that Millarca and Carmilla are one and the same, both incarnations of a famous vampire, Countess

Karnstein, who died years ago. (There is some indication of this earlier in the novel, when a portrait of Countess Karnstein is seen, and it is pointed out that it exactly resembles Carmilla, down to a tiny mole on her neck.) Laura's father vows to find and kill Carmilla, and after a dramatic showdown with the cornered vampire in a ruined chapel, a vampire specialist, Baron Vordenburg, is sent for. He manages to find the Countess's tomb, exhumes the body, and performs the appropriate vampire-slaying rituals. Carmilla is destroyed for ever, and young Laura is saved from the vampire's deathly embrace.

Lesbian love

Le Fanu's *Carmilla* was a sensation. It clearly derived much of its excitement from the unspoken passion between the two young women, in scenes that were couched

in the euphemistic language of the day, but which were quite clearly sexual in nature. In an age where young women spent a great deal of time together, often without male company, such feelings were bound to evoke great curiosity, particularly from female readers.

This aspect of the vampire myth, particularly in its portrayal of lust as a deathly form of greed, in which the aroused lover wants to consume the loved one, had never before been expressed so directly in gothic fiction. From this point on, the vampire becomes an iconic image of the sexually voracious individual, whether male or female, seeking to destroy the object of its passion by feasting on its flesh and drinking its blood. In this way, the myth begins to explore and express the controlling, destructive aspect of human sexuality. What was particularly shocking about Carmilla was that this covert discussion took place in the taboo context of lesbian love, and that the author attributed such intense sexual feelings to women as well as men.

Le Fanu was undoubtedly influenced in his writing by the French scholar Augustin Calmet's work on vampires and revenants. This had been translated into English under the title of *The Phantom World* some years prior to the publication of *Carmilla*. In addition, Le Fanu is thought to have consulted Sabine Baring Gould's *Book of Werewolves*, published in 1863, Samuel Taylor Coleridge's narrative poem *Christabel*, and *Schloss Hainfeld*, an account by Captain Basil Hall of the Royal Navy, telling of a winter spent in Lower Styria, Austria.

Carmilla was to have a lasting legacy in vampire literature. It greatly influenced the most famous novel of the genre, Bram Stoker's *Dracula*, and was also said to have inspired parts of Henry James's *The Turn of the Screw*.

Bram Stoker's Dracula

One of the most significant aspects of *Carmilla*, from today's perspective, is that it was a forerunner of Bram Stoker's *Dracula*. Although *Dracula* was a much longer and more elaborate novel than *Carmilla*, the influence of the former work is evident in several ways. In the first draft of *Dracula*, seven years prior to final publication in 1897, the Count's remote castle is set, like Le Fanu's castle, in Styria, Austria. Later, this was altered, and Stoker made Transylvania the setting of the book. There are also many similarities between the characters of Carmilla and Lucy, Stoker's central female vampire figure. Both are beautiful women who are not only very desirable to others, but who themselves have strong sexual desires. In addition to these important similarities, the 'vampire expert' in Stoker's novel, Professor Abraham Van Helsing, bears more than a passing resemblance to Le Fanu's vampire slayer, Baron Vordenburg.

Gothic fantasy

Dracula was an extremely significant novel that, after a relatively slow start, captured the public imagination and has provided the template for vampire horror fiction ever since. Contemporary commentators have pointed out that today, *Dracula* is regarded as a classic work of fiction, largely as the result of the attention drawn to it by the many film versions of the book that appeared in the twentieth century; however,

at the time of its publication, it was seen by the majority of the public simply as an enjoyable adventure story. There were Victorian critics who recognized its seminal, iconic status, comparing it to other outstanding novels in the horror genre, such as Mary Shelley's *Frankenstein*, but in general, these reviewers were few and far between.

Abraham Stoker was the personal assistant of Henry Irving, a well-known actor and the owner of the Lyceum Theatre in London. Besides his work for Irving, Stoker was also a prolific writer of novels and short stories. As a denizen of the London theatre, Stoker understood better than most the popular taste for dramatic action, high adventure, and gothic fantasy, and used this knowledge to make his fiction appealing to readers.

Bram, as he was generally known, had been brought up in County Donegal, the third son of seven children. His mother, Charlotte Thornely, was an early feminist. The family were cultured but not well off, and as a child Stoker suffered a great deal of illness. He was bedridden until the age of seven. During this time, his mother used to read to him and tell him ghost stories; he was an imaginative child, and, as he put it, 'the leisure of long illness gave opportunity for many thoughts which were fruitful ... in later years.'

COLLECTION LITTÉRAIRE DES
ROMANS ÉTRANGERS

BRAHM STOKER

DRACULA
L'HOMME DE LA NUIT

Traduit par Ève et Lucie PAUL-MARGUERITTE

4ᵐᵉ mille

L'ÉDITION FRANÇAISE ILLUSTRÉE
PARIS — 3o, RUE DE PROVENCE, 3o — PARIS

Front cover of the French edition of *Dracula* by Bram Stoker, 1920.

Science and superstition

At the age of seven, Bram made a miraculous recovery, completed his education, and went on to study at Trinity College, Dublin. He then became a theatre critic for a local paper. After reviewing a performance of *Hamlet* by Henry Irving, he and Irving became friends. Later, Stoker and his wife moved to London, where he began to work for Irving, whom he had now come to idolize. (He even named his only son after Irving.)

An intelligent, cultured man, Stoker read widely and had many interests, including the study of folklore, science, medicine, criminology, and the occult. He was also fascinated by mesmerism – a theraputic technique involving hypnotism. He had great faith in the power of science over irrationalism and superstition, which is ironic considering that he created the most famous evil vampire character in English literature. However, one could argue that the aim of *Dracula* was ultimately to help dispel the vampire myth once and for all. Moreover, some critics have pointed out that by the end of the nineteenth century, superstitious pagan beliefs among urban populations – at least in England – had receded to the point where it became possible to approach ideas of the supernatural in a more playful, entertaining way.

Gary Oldman in Francis Ford Coppola's *Dracula*, 1992.

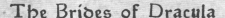
The Brides of Dracula

Stoker wrote *Dracula* as a series of letters, journal entries, and newspaper clippings made by several narrators, which allowed him the scope to tell the story from different points of view. The adventure concerns a young solicitor, Jonathan Harker's visit to his client, Count Dracula, who lives in a remote castle in the Carpathian Mountains. Harker finds his host gracious and welcoming, but realizes after a while that he has become trapped in the castle. Count Dracula tries to find out as much information as he can about London, Harker's home city, and we get the impression that Dracula plans to visit the city soon.

In the meantime, the Count warns Harker not to wander around the castle at night, but Harker does so, trying to escape. He is set upon by three licentious women, The Brides of Dracula, who, as it transpires, are vampires. They attack Harker, who is saved at the last minute by the Count. Eventually, Harker makes his escape, returning to London and the company of his faithful fiancée, Mina Murray, and her friend, the vivacious Lucy Westenra.

Unbeknown to Harker, Dracula makes the journey to London from his castle in Transylvania, and begins to prey on the local populace. Not long afterwards, Lucy falls prey to a mysterious disease. Doctors are called in, including one Professor Abraham Van Helsing from Holland. Van Helsing immediately suspects that Lucy has been bitten by a vampire, but does not communicate his fears, instead treating his patient with blood transfusions. On the night Van Helsing returns to Amsterdam, Lucy and her mother are attacked by a huge wolf. Both women, tragically, die shortly afterwards.

Stabbed in the throat

After Lucy's burial, reports in the newspaper describe a beautiful woman who stalks children by night. Van Helsing reads these reports and realizes that Lucy has now become a vampire. He and Lucy's various suitors go to her grave and destroy her vampiric self by exhuming her body, cutting off her head, putting a stake through her heart, and filling her mouth with garlic.

However, Mina then becomes ill, and it transpires that she has developed a telepathic connection with Count Dracula, who has been wandering about London, and has visited her at night, feeding her his blood. Through Mina, who is hypnotized by Professor Van Helsing, the men track Dracula's movements as he flees back to his castle in Transylvania. Finally, they catch up with him, just before nightfall, and stab him in the throat and heart. Count Dracula crumbles to dust and the spell is lifted.

Of all Stoker's many sensationalist novels, *Dracula* became the most successful. Its theme of an English invasion by a foreign force, in this case Count Dracula's visit to London, chimed with a number of other important novels on a similar theme, by writers such as Arthur Conan Doyle, H.G. Wells, Rudyard Kipling, and Rider Haggard, concerning terrifying mythical creatures invading Britain from abroad. Commentators today have argued that *Dracula* drew much of its appeal from the idea that England was being influenced by corrupting forces from the continent; according to this argument, the image of the bloodsucking Austrian Count is symbolic of the gradual infiltration of degenerate influences from abroad.

> ### HE CREATED THE MOST FAMOUS EVIL VAMPIRE CHARACTER IN ENGLISH LITERATURE

The model for Count Dracula

As with John Polidori's vampire, Count Dracula was an aristocratic figure. In Polidori's case, he drew on the character of Lord Byron for inspiration. In Stoker's, he used his boss, the charismatic Henry Irving, as a model for the vampire. Although talented, gracious, and charming, Irving could also be tyrannical and domineering, and it was the contrast between these two aspects of the same character that made Stoker's fictional vampire so fascinating. Count Dracula expressed a deep dichotomy in human nature, that is, the existence of primitive, aggressive, destructive sexual drives alongside the cultured, refined personality.

In addition, the character of Van Helsing presented the paradox between science and irrationalism, in that the Professor is at once a well-educated medical man, with a vast knowledge of science, and at the same time has an extensive understanding of the darker forces of human nature, which includes vampirism. This theme of the dual personality, and the role of science in understanding the workings of the irrational unconscious mind, had previously been a theme in other Victorian stories and novels, such as Robert Louis Stevenson's *The Strange Case of Dr Jekyll and Mr Hyde*, published in 1886.

The Order of the Dragon

There is some controversy as to the historical inspiration for the central character of Stoker's Count Dracula. Some point to the infamous fifteenth century Prince of Wallachia, Vlad III, who was known as Vlad Tepes (meaning 'Vlad the Impaler'). This ruler had a reputation as one of the most bloodthirsty men that ever lived, and was said to have killed hundreds of thousands of people by impaling them on sharp poles (see page 99). His cruelty was legendary throughout Europe, but many Romanians saw him as a hero, since he had defended them from Turkish Muslims who wanted to invade the country.

The formidable Vlad III also had another name, commonly used by his people – Dracula. Vlad's father had been a member of a secret order of knights called the Order of the Dragon. This was founded by King Sigismund of Hungary, who later became the Holy Roman Emperor, its purpose being to fight the enemies of Christianity. Vlad II took up this cause with a vengeance, so much so that he became known to his subjects as 'dracul' – the dragon. His son Vlad III then became known as 'dracula' – son of 'dracul'.

According to various sources, including Stoker's notes, the first draft of the novel featured a man named Count Wampyr as the main character. This was later changed to Dracula when Stoker came across the name during his research. However, it is not clear whether Stoker actually knew very much about the original Vlad the Impaler when he chose this name for his vampire; it may be that he simply liked the sound of it. Whatever the case, in his novel, Stoker made no reference to the fact that the Count had impaled thousands of hapless victims, nor that he had been involved in an ongoing battle with the Turks for control of his country (which, in Stoker's account, is Transylvania, not Romania).

Bathing in blood

Other scholars point to Countess Elizabeth Báthory, the sixteenth-century Hungarian aristocrat famous for torturing and murdering hundreds of young women in

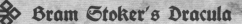

her castle, as a possible model for Count Dracula. In particular, there were rumours – some believe entirely unfounded – that the Countess liked to bathe in her victims' blood, in the hope that this would help her to retain her youth (see page 113). A similar theme emerges in Stoker's book, when the Count is said to look younger after a feed of blood. However, this connection appears to be somewhat tenuous, since in many other accounts, vampires are said to be rejuvenated by the blood of their victims.

To this day, it is not clear exactly where Stoker derived the inspiration for his Count Dracula, but it seems likely that he was influenced by a combination of ideas, derived from his extensive research into European folklore and history.

Gary Oldman

Gary Oldman is a British actor whose memorable performance in *Dracula* directed by Francis Ford Coppola (1992) earned him a permanent place in vampire movie history. A highly versatile actor, he nevertheless made the role of the Count his own, and attracted many plaudits as a result.

A shameless hussy

While some regard Stoker's *Dracula* as a rather crude, sensationalist novel, there is no doubt that it touches on some profound themes. First and foremost, Stoker explores the struggle between the modernizing forces of science and technology and the dark, primitive currents of pagan belief that were still alive in rural parts of Europe during the Victorian period. His character Van Helsing seems to give credence to both these approaches, on the one hand using modern medical techniques such as blood transfusions to cure his patient, and on the other employing age-old remedies such as hanging a necklace of garlic flowers around her neck, to ward off vampires. At a time when investigations into psychology were only just beginning to be taken seriously, Stoker presents innovative ideas about the healing power of the mind, and the ways that medical science can harness this power (for example, through hypnotism).

Secondly, the book is concerned with another issue of great importance to Victorian society, that is to say, the changing role of women. In particular, the issue of female sexuality is addressed, though in a less than progressive way. In the story, we witness the gradual corruption of Lucy from a lively, popular, and attractive young virgin into a shameless hussy. Lucy is depicted as having many suitors, and as enjoying the attention paid to her by all of them, until she finally chooses a husband. There is an inference that her interest in men, combined with her beauty, leads her to her eventual ruin, in the shape of becoming a sexually aggressive, lustful vampire. By contrast, Mina, the other woman in the story, is presented as feminine and maternal, devoted to her husband, Harker; the implication is that, as a consequence, she is saved the wanton Lucy's terrible fate.

The fate of Count Dracula

Bram Stoker, it is generally believed, had high hopes that his patron Henry Irving would play the role of Count Dracula in a stage adaptation of the novel. Irving, however, who regarded himself as a champion of the theatre as a highbrow art form, was dismissive of the idea, much to Stoker's disappointment. Stoker's dream was never realized before Irving died in 1905. In 1912, Stoker himself died, after a series of strokes, which some biographers have attributed to syphilis. Despite his many literary efforts, he had made relatively little money in his life, and most of his work was soon forgotten.

It was left to Stoker's widow Florence to publish a posthumous short story collection, *Dracula's Guest and Other Weird Stories*,

two years after his death. In 1922, Stoker's novel *Dracula* was adapted for the screen, prompting Mrs Stoker to sue the director Friedrich Wilhelm Murnau, through the British Society of Authors. She claimed that she had never given permission for the story to be filmed, and had not been paid a single penny in royalties for it. In July 1925, having battled determinedly with the film makers, the courts finally decided in favour of Mrs Stoker.

Despite the fact that during the legal battle, Mrs Stoker demanded the destruction of all prints of the film, some copies survived. Murnau's *Dracula* has since become a milestone in the history of horror cinema, also attracting attention to the classic novel on which it was based.

Modern Vampire Fiction

Throughout the twentieth century, the vampire myth continued to endure, largely because of the many horror films about the subject that were released from the 1920s onward (see below, page 166). These proved immensely popular with the public, relying as they did on the exciting visual elements of gothic horror, including various new technologies in the cinema, such as dramatic special effects. However, despite these innovations, the literary vampire was not forgotten. Science fiction, horror, and romance novels featuring vampires continued to sell, sometimes inspiring screen versions, at other times inspired by the film themselves; and today, the genre has become more popular than ever, with the tremendous success of Stephenie Meyer's teenage horror/romance vampire series, *Twilight*.

I Am Legend

One of the most influential science fiction novels of the 1950s was *I Am Legend* by Richard Matheson. This imaginative novel told the story of the sole survivor of a terrible plague that had killed off most of humankind. The plague, as the protagonist finds out, was caused by a little-known type of bacteria that fed off live bodies as well as dead ones, and caused affected people to show symptoms of vampirism. What we find out as the book progresses is that only the dead corpses reanimated by the bacteria are true vampires; the others are ordinary human beings afflicted by a terrible disease that, like rabies, changes their personalities and behaviour.

In the story, the hero, Robert Neville, recovers from a serious illness to find that all other human beings in the vicinity have vanished. Instead, a vampire horde, some of whom are former friends, besiege his house each night, terrifying him with their aggressive behaviour. He does his best to repel them, and manages to kill several of the vampires. In his efforts to keep them at bay, he boards up his windows and hangs up garlic. During the daylight hours, he spends much of his time disposing of dead vampire bodies. Not surprisingly, given the fact that his life has become a living hell, he begins to suffer from depression. He also starts to drink heavily. However, little by little, through patient research using books from the local library, he learns the truth about the disease and realizes he has escaped a terrible fate. The twist in the tale of the novel is that, since he is the only person on earth who has survived uncontaminated, ultimately it is he, not the mass of humanity, who has become the 'odd one out', and who will have to pay the price, becoming a 'legend' from the past, like the vampire itself.

Neville meets a woman, Ruth, who appears to have escaped the plague, but he soon begins to suspect that she, too, has been infected. He tries to give her a blood test, but they struggle, and she knocks him out. He awakes to find a note from Ruth explaining that the now-infected members of the human race are struggling to rebuild their civilization. Neville has failed to distinguish between the dead who have been reactivated by the disease (the true 'vampires') and infected humans, and has killed some members of their community; thus, he has become hated and feared by the infected humans, who now form the majority of the human race. The infected humans are struggling to adapt to their condition, and are beginning to find ways of keeping the true vampires at bay. Ruth warns him in the note that he must leave his home, as the infected horde will come to capture him there.

Biological Freak

Weary and defeated, Neville decides to stay put, and gives himself up to his captors. In prison, while awaiting execution, he is visited by Ruth, who slips him some suicide pills. He goes to the window and sees the crowd outside, waiting for him with fear and horror in their eyes. At this moment, he realizes that he has become a monster to them, just as they were to him; the infected are now the mainstream of society, and it is he, not them, who is deviant. He decides to swallow the pills, in the knowledge that for them, he has now become a throwback, a frightening creature from the past, who has no place in this new world. As he dies, he laughs bitterly, realizing that he will now become a legend, a horror story, a biological freak, that will terrify this new human race.

I Am Legend expressed, as did much science fiction of the period, aspects of social anxiety caused by the repressive mores of the Cold War years: in particular the treatment of those seen as outside the social norm, and the fear of unorthodoxy as a kind of 'disease' that might infiltrate the mainstream. Horror writer Stephen King has spoken of the influence that the book had on him. But the book's most lasting legacy has been in the world of film: in 1964, it was adapted under the title, *The Last Man on Earth*; in 1971 it appeared on screen as *The Omega Man*; and in 2007, it was remade under its original name, *I Am Legend*.

Charlton Heston in the 1971 adaptation of *I Am Legend*, *The Omega Man*.

Tom Cruise

Tom Cruise starred as the vampire Lestat de Lioncourt in 1994's *Interview with the Vampire: The Vampire Chronicles*, directed by Neil Jordan and based on Anne Rice's bestseller. The casting of such a clean-cut, all-American actor in the role of the gaunt, suave Lestat, attracted criticism in some quarters, but the film went on to win many awards.

Brad Pitt

Brad Pitt also played a vampire in *Interview*, taking the role of Louis de Pointe du Lac alongside Cruise, and recounting his 200-year-old life story, including his initiation into vampirism by Lestat. The film was a box-office success, and brought Rice's novels back into the bestseller lists.

The Vampire Chronicles

Although there were various vampire novels throughout the sixties, such as the Marilyn Ross series featuring Barnabas Collins (see page 172), these were mostly spin-offs from films or TV series. However, in 1976, Anne Rice established the vampire horror novel as a new genre with her landmark debut, *Interview with the Vampire*.

Rice was born Howard Allen O'Brien and grew up in New Orleans in an Irish-American Catholic family. She was named after her father, but re-named herself Anne on her first day at school. She attended university in Texas and then moved to San Francisco, where she worked as an insurance claims investigator before marrying her childhood sweetheart, Stan Rice. The couple had two children, Michelle and Christopher. Michelle died of leukaemia at the age of four. An avid writer, Rice completed her first novel, *Interview with the Vampire* in 1973. Three years later it was published, becoming the first in a long and extremely successful series known as *The Vampire Chronicles*, continuing until 2003.

Burned by sunlight

The central character in the novel is a 200-year-old vampire, Louis, who relates the story in the first person, giving it a unique perspective. Louis tells how, in 1791, a vampire called Lestat de Lioncourt turned him into a vampire, and the pair became friends for eternity. Louis, for moral reasons, cannot feed off humans, and only drinks the blood of animals; little by little he becomes more critical of his friend Lestat's vampire ways, and considers going it alone, only to find that Lestat has procured a vampire 'daughter' for them, a child he calls Claudia.

Because of her status as a vampire, Claudia must remain a child for the rest of her life. Louis grows to hate Lestat, and kills him, leaving him for dead, but Lestat returns to attack him. Louis and Claudia manage to escape, travelling to Europe, where Louis turns a Parisian dollmaker, Madeleine, into a vampire mother for Claudia. Eventually, Lestat catches up with them, and Madeleine and Claudia die, burned to death by daylight. Louis manages to travel on, but ends his days as a lonely man.

In telling the story, Rice introduced several variations on the classic vampire myth, which were elaborated on further in *Chronicles*. Her vampires were not destroyed or deterred by crucifixes, garlic, wooden stakes, and so on. They were sensitive, gifted individuals with magical powers, such as the ability to read thoughts and move objects by mind control. The most powerful of them were a thousand years old, and had supernatural features such as the ability to

influence a person's will, and superhuman sight, hearing, and strength. In some cases, the vampires could fly. They could also set an object or person on fire, or cause a person to have a fatal heart attack. Most significantly, all had the potential of eternal life, and were subject only to death by fire, sunlight, or a more powerful vampire's attack. If they were wounded, they healed rapidly, and could regenerate themselves. The oldest vampires were extremely powerful, and as they aged, their skin whitened to a marble-like appearance.

The torture of eternal life

However, Rice makes it clear that, for her vampires, this gift of immortality is in some ways a curse. After a 100 or 200 years, vampires become tired and unhappy, and may exhibit signs of mental instability. They may try to take their own lives, or go into hibernation to avoid the sheer tedium of living. Rice emphasizes that eternal life is a kind of torture for most of them, provoking a kind of existential despair that cannot even be extinguished by death.

The tone of *Interview with the Vampire* is sombre, and Rice has said that the mood of it was influenced by her daughter's death from leukaemia. It continues to be regarded by many critics as her best book, and in 1994, was made into a major film starring Tom Cruise, Brad Pitt and Kirsten Dunst. Later books, *The Vampire Lestat* and *The Queen of the Damned*, were filmed under the latter title in 2002. These films, especially *Interview with the Vampire*, brought renewed interest in Rice's work, so much so that to date, her books have sold nearly one hundred million copies. Today, despite the fact that some critics have argued that the later novels in the series lack the originality of *Interview*, she continues to be one of the most widely read authors in the world.

Vampire Novels

The Vampyre

By John Polidori (1819). Polidori was Lord Byron's friend and physician, and his story was inspired by a fragment written by the famous romantic poet. Polidori's great innovation was to change the vampire from a medieval monster dripping with gore to a refined aristocrat: the pale, seductive Lord Ruthven.

Carmilla

By Joseph Sheridan Le Fanu (1872). Le Fanu was the greatest ghost story writer of the Victorian era. In *Carmilla*, a Gothic novella, he turned his attention to the vampire myth, with a sensational tale of love between a young woman and a female vampire that shocked his readers.

Dracula

By Bram Stoker (1897). This is the novel that started the vampire craze. Stoker was an Irish writer who drew on real historical figures, such as Vlad the Impaler, and European mythology, to create the tale of Count Dracula, who lures his victims to their doom in his Transylvanian castle.

I Am Legend

By Richard Matheson (1954). This highly influential novel mixed horror with science fiction, telling the story of how one man fights a plague of disease-ridden vampires who threaten to destroy human life on earth. The theme of apocalypse proved to be very popular in cold-war America.

Salem's Lot

By Stephen King (1975). The second of King's novels, *Salem's Lot* tells the story of a writer who comes back to his hometown in Maine, only to find it threatened by vampires. It's a classic King tale about evil flourishing in the very midst of suburban normality.

The Vampire Chronicles

By Anne Rice (1976-2003). *Interview with the Vampire* was the first in a series chronicling the life of Lestat de Liancourt, an eighteenth-century French nobleman, and his many subsequent incarnations. The Chronicles is one of the most successful vampire series of all time, with sales of over 80 million.

The Hunger

By Whitley Strieber (1981). Miriam Blaylock is a beautiful female vampire who takes human lovers and transforms them into hybrid vampire/humans, disposing of them when she is tired of them. Strieber describes vampires as a species akin to humans, with a set of practical problems such as how to acquire and dispose of bodies.

They Thirst

By Robert McCammon (1981). This novel imagines a horror scenario in which Los Angeles is taken over by vampires, transforming it into a city of the dead. The novel is currently out of print, and McCammon regards it as inferior to his later works, and has refused to let it be reprinted.

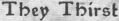

Fevre Dream

By George R.R. Martin (1982). This highly regarded historical novel is set in Mississippi in the mid-nineteenth century. A tale of steamboats, vampire hunters, and the darker side of New Orleans, it has been described as 'Bram Stoker meets Mark Twain', and continues to attract awards.

The Stress of Her Regard

By Tim Powers (1989). Lord Byron, Percy Shelley, Mary Shelley, John Keats, and John Polidori feature in this novel, which imagines that these real historical figures were members of a vampire-like clan of succubi, lamia, fairies and other mythological creatures – some of them evil, but others good.

Anita Blake: Vampire Hunter

By Laurell Kaye Hamilton (1993-present). This bestselling series, about a female necromancer turned magical investigator, began with the first novel, *Guilty Pleasures*, and in the twenty-seven novels thereafter has continued to attract readers with its focus on the erotic side of the vampire myth.

The Last Vampire

By Christopher Pike (1994-2013). This series chronicles the life of a 5,000-year-old vampire, Sita, drawing from ancient history and world mythology as well from the science fiction and horror genres. Christopher Pike is a bestselling author of young adult and children's fiction, whose real name is Kevin McFadden.

The Southern Vampire Mysteries

Series by Charlaine Harris (2001-2013). *Dead Until Dark*, the first novel in the series, introduces Sookie Stackhouse, a telepathic waitress in the small town of Bon Temps, Louisiana, who falls in love with a handsome vampire and embarks on solving a series of murders in the town. The basis for the *True Blood* TV series.

Vampire Kisses

By Ellen Schreiber (2003-2009). The series begins by introducing us to Raven Madison, a sixteen-year-old who complains that her life is boring. However, when a stranger, vampire Alexander Sterling, comes to town, she falls in love and embarks on a series of adventures in the world of the supernatural.

Twilight

By Stephenie Meyer (2005-2008). The latest vampire series sensation, the novels chart the adventures of teenager Bella Swan, who falls in love with a classmate, vampire Edward Cullen, thus endangering her life. Hailed as a thoughtful reflection on teenage sexuality, the books have sold millions of copies worldwide.

The 'Twilight' Series

One of the most extraordinary developments in modern vampire fiction has taken place in the new millennium, with the publication of Stephenie Meyer's *Twilight* series of novels for the teen market. The first of these, the eponymous *Twilight*, appeared in 2005, and there have since been three more in the series: *New Moon*, published in 2006, *Eclipse*, in 2007, and *Breaking Dawn*, in 2008. A film adaptation of *Twilight*, released in 2008, has increased the already astronomical sales of the original novel, and the second film, *New Moon*, released in November 2009, is continuing to build on the series' success.

Teenage sexuality

The author, Stephenie Meyer, tells of how the idea for the story of *Twilight*, that of a vampire who falls in love with a teenage girl but thirsts for her blood, came to her in a dream one night. Evidently, in terms of human psychology, this is a very strong scenario, since it touches on the intense sexuality of the teenager, expressing on the one hand, the anxiety young men of this age may feel about harming a girl that they are emotionally attached to, and on the other, the mixture of fear and excitement that a young woman may feel about losing her virginity. Although the story was ostensibly about a mythical world – that of the vampire – it appealed to young adults because it described so vividly the real sexual and emotional anxieties of the teenage years, including feelings of alienation from society; of being 'different'; of one's burgeoning sexuality being harmful, even fatal, to others; of struggling to come to terms with the adult world of responsibility; of being doomed to failure; and so on.

The story of *Twilight* introduces the central character, Isabella Swan, known as Bella. As a teenager, Bella moves from her home in Phoenix, Arizona, to live with her father, Charlie, in Forks, Washington, while her mother and stepfather go travelling. Thus, she leaves behind the sunshine of her childhood years, and begins to make her way in a confusing, and complex, adult world.

Forbidden fruit

On her first day at her new school, she meets a handsome young man, Edward Cullen. Later, when she is almost run over in the parking lot at school, Cullen manages to save her, showing superhuman strength by stopping the van with his bare hands. Bella is intrigued, and tries to find out more about him, eventually learning that he and his family are vampires. Instead of human blood, they drink animal blood.

The plot thickens when other vampires come to town, including a vampire called James, who wants to attack Bella. Bella tries to escape from James, but eventually he catches up with her, and bites her. Edward comes to the rescue, destroying James, and sucking out the venom from James' bite before it can infect Bella and turn her into a vampire. Bella is grateful to Edward, but at the school prom, she tells him that she wants to become a vampire. Although Edward loves her, he refuses, knowing the difficulties that such a life will bring her.

As a metaphor for sexual development in modern-day teenagers, the novel works well.

Although the young couple have intense feelings for one another, they cannot engage in a sexual relationship, as this would corrupt Bella and she would become a vampire. Sexual love is seen as a 'forbidden fruit'.

As regards the modern world, the story of *Twilight* seems to express some important themes. It recognizes that, contrary to sensational media coverage, many teenagers in actual fact approach the idea of sex with caution, and may sometimes feel they do not want to sully a 'pure' love relationship through having sex. In a society where the dangers of pregnancy and sexually transmitted diseases are constantly discussed in the media, and where sex is often represented as a cheap commodity, it is not surprising that sensitive and intelligent young people might have such a reaction. In addition, in the United States, there is a strong 'chastity before marriage' movement in some religious sections of the population. It seems that, since the days of sexual liberation in the sixties and seventies, and with the onset of AIDS in the eighties, the picture for many adolescents has changed, so that the complexities and dangers of early sexual relationships, as well as the pleasures, are given more consideration. And, for all its gothic elements of romance and horror, the *Twilight* series appears to recognize these concerns, which perhaps explains the stories' current appeal to teenagers across the world.

Robert Pattinson

Robert Pattinson took on the mantle of handsome young vampire Edward Cullen in the film adaptation of *Twilight*, based on the Stephenie Meyer novel, becoming a heart-throb for the millions of teenage girls who saw the film. He also contributed as a singer and co-composer on some of the music for the soundtrack.

Vampires on Screen

Since the early twentieth century, the figure of the vampire has inspired countless films, some of them classics. These films have influenced popular conceptions of the vampire legend, adding many features, for example, introducing the notion that vampires fear daylight, have fangs, and sport high-collared cloaks, which are not essential part of the original folklore.

Femmes fatales

Early screen vampires, in the days of silent films, were not literally bloodsucking fiends, but seductive women, known as 'vamps', or femmes fatales. These early screen sirens preyed on foolish men – and their wallets. The films include *The Vampire* (1913) and *A Fool There Was* (1915) starring Theda Bara. No actual vampire appeared until 1922, when F.W. Murnau made *Nosferatu*, based on the novel by Bram Stoker (for more information on this, see page 150).

In 1931, the first vampire 'talkie' was released: *Dracula*, starring Bela Lugosi. With his slow, menacing speech and deathly pallor, Lugosi personified the living corpse, and frightened audiences so much that some fainted with shock when they saw him. The film was a box-office sensation and for many, Lugosi became the definitive Count Dracula. Two sequels followed, *Dracula's Daughter* (1936), and *Son of Dracula* (1943). The fact that the Count had been well and truly destroyed in the first film did not stop him coming to life again for further Hollywood horrors, including *House of Frankenstein* (1944), *House of Dracula* (1945), and a comedy, *Abbot and Costello Meet Frankenstein* (1948).

The making of Dracula

The *Dracula* film of 1931 was directed by Tod Browning and was based on a stage play by Hamilton Deane and John L. Balderston, which in turn drew inspiration from the original book by Bram Stoker. The play was already a big Broadway hit, and provided the producers with a blueprint for the film version. Bela Lugosi, a Hungarian actor, was cast in the central part, but there were reservations about this choice, and he had to accept a lower salary than many of his co-stars. Legend has it that Lugosi could hardly speak English when he made the film, which accounted for his heavy accent; however, this seems unlikely, since he had been working in Hollywood for some time by this point.

There are many stories about the making of the film, including the rumour that Tod Browning took no interest in the process, and that as a consequence there was a great deal of chaos on set. It appears that Browning was upset by the death from cancer of his friend Lon Chaney, who would have been picked to play the part of the Count. Nevertheless, despite all these difficulties, the film became a milestone in the cinema, not least because it showed how the industry moved from the 'silent' era to the 'talkies'. In contrast to today's films, there were many silent moments during the movie, and most of the actors' lines were brief and to the point. The script limited itself to explaining the story, rather than developing the characters' relationships through dialogue, and in this sense, although a 'talkie', the film's structure bore a strong resemblance to that of the silent movies.

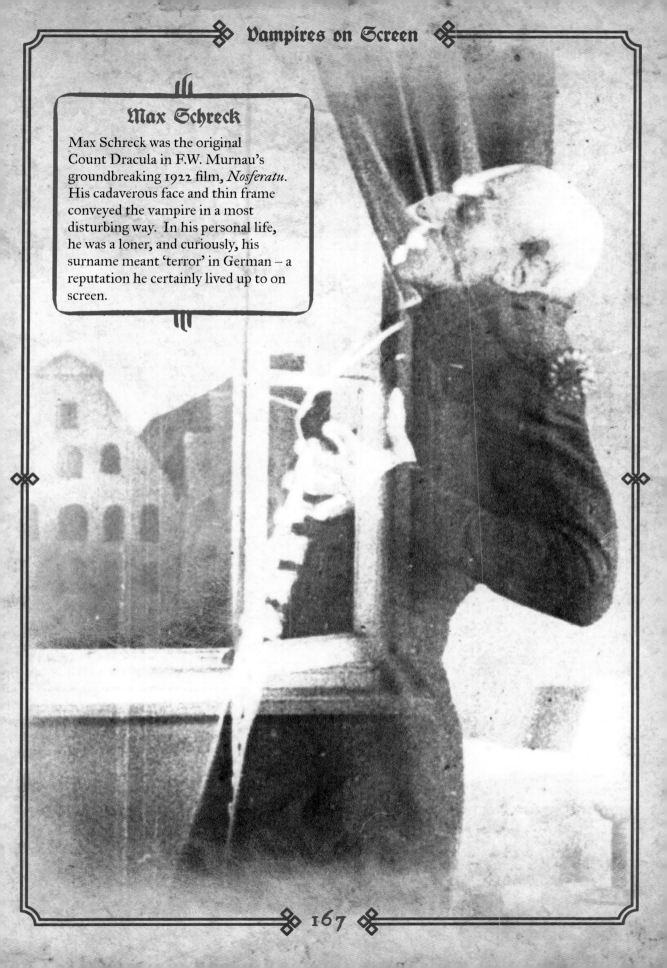

Max Schreck

Max Schreck was the original Count Dracula in F.W. Murnau's groundbreaking 1922 film, *Nosferatu*. His cadaverous face and thin frame conveyed the vampire in a most disturbing way. In his personal life, he was a loner, and curiously, his surname meant 'terror' in German – a reputation he certainly lived up to on screen.

The TERRIFYING Lover –
who died – yet lived !

Universal-International presents A Hammer Film Production

PETER CUSHING in

DRACULA

(Cert. **X**) Adults only

Also starring **MICHAEL GOUGH**
and **MELISSA STRIBLING**
With **CHRISTOPHER LEE** as Dracula

In Eastman Colour processed by Technicolor

Screenplay by JIMMY SANGSTER   Associate Producer ANTHONY NELSON-KEYS
Produced by ANTHONY HINDS   Directed by TERENCE FISHER
Executive Producer MICHAEL CARRERAS

  Distributed by Rank Film Distributors Ltd.

The premiere of *Dracula* took place on Valentine's Day in 1931. The studio took care to circulate stories of the extraordinary effect it had on those present at the screening, including tales of people being carried out of the cinema suffering from shock. This drew large audiences to the cinema to see it, more perhaps from curiosity than anything else. It proved to be a huge hit, which was by no means a foregone conclusion at the time. Today, it is listed in the Library of Congress as a film of 'cultural, historical and aesthetic significance'. For Lugosi, however, it was a mixed blessing; from that point, he was typecast as Count Dracula, and never again played a wide variety of parts.

Medieval monsters

Even though the portrait of the vampire as an elegant, cultured aristocrat with a decadent taste for blood triumphed in the cinema, the medieval monster of Slavic folklore was not entirely forgotten. Inspired by F. W. Murnau's groundbreaking *Nosferatu* in the twenties, German director Werner Herzog followed up with *Nosferatu the Vampyre* (1979), a homage to, and update of, the original film, which Herzog considered to be the greatest film ever to come out of his country. In Herzog's film, the vampire is portrayed as a hideous, lonely creature to be pitied rather than admired. Other vampire films with this theme include Elias Merhige's *Shadow of the Vampire* (2000), a fictional account of the making of Murnau's film, in which the lead actor turns out to be a vampire, much to the horror of the cast and crew.

The Hammer Horrors

In the fifties, the Dracula legend continued with the British Hammer Horror series. The first of these, *Dracula* (retitled in the US as *Horror of Dracula*) was released in 1958 and starred Christopher Lee as the Count. With an incredibly low budget of just over £80,000 the film nevertheless managed to capture the public imagination, and became an instant success, spawning seven sequels. Tall, dark and gruesome, Lee brought a chilling suavity and magnetic sex appeal to the role that thrilled cinema audiences throughout the following decade.

Christopher Lee

Christopher Lee (right) was the star of the Hammer Horror series of vampire films, and is regarded as one of the best cinema vampires of all time. He played the Count as a cultured, refined aristocrat, but managed to convey a sense of deep evil too, as well as a wicked sense of humour.

The sixties and seventies saw a proliferation of vampire films covering all kinds of subjects, from sex to comedy to science fiction. There were a number of lesbian vampire films loosely based on Le Fanu's *Carmilla* (see page 147), including Roger Vadim's *Blood and Roses* (1960), *The Vampire Lovers* (1970), and *Vampyres* (1974). Among the many comedy films was Roman Polanski's entertaining send-up of the genre, *The Fearless Vampire Killers* (1967), and *Love at First Bite* (1979) starring David Niven. Several science fiction films, such as *The Omega Man* (1971) took their cue from Richard Matheson's vampire novel *I Am Legend* (see page 158).

As the seventies progressed, the themes became more diverse: there was even a film about race, the blaxploitation movie *Blacula* (1972). One subject, however, continued to be a stable box-office draw: the vampire as sex symbol. By the eighties and nineties, a number of gay pornographic movies were being made, including *Gayracula* (1983). In the new millennium, the trend continued *Lust for Dracula* (2005), a lesbian remake of Bram Stoker's classic.

Barnabas Collins

From 1966 to 1971, the ABC TV series *Dark Shadows* introduced audiences to a 'sympathetic' vampire. Barnabas, played by actor Jonathan Frid, is from an eighteenth century family, and has had an affair with his fiancée's maid, Angelique. Angelique has cast a powerful spell on him, using voodoo. After a series of setbacks, Barnabas shoots Angelique, who summons a demon bat from hell to attack him. Angelique recovers, but Barnabas dies, only to rise again from the grave as a vampire, forever searching for his true love. Wracked by self-loathing and misery, Barnabas the vampire brings more chaos and despair to his family, and

eventually asks his father Joshua to kill him. Joshua feels unable to oblige, and instead asks Barnabas' devoted former servant Ben to do the deed. Ben puts a crucifix inside Barnabas' coffin and wraps it round with chains. The coffin is then placed in the family mausoleum, where it stays for many years.

In ensuing episodes, Barnabas comes to life again, when a man named Willie Loomis comes to the Collins family crypt to look for lost jewels, and accidentally releases Barnabas from the coffin. More mayhem ensues as Barnabas falls in love with a young woman, Maggie Evans, and tries to make her his vampire bride; Maggie escapes but is traumatized by the experience and loses her mind. She is treated by Dr Julia Hoffman, who also tries to help Barnabas. The plots continued, with many twists and turns in true soap-opera style, until the series finally came to an end in 1971.

The lovelorn vampire

The *Dark Shadows* series drew on many aspects of vampire mythology, including the idea that Barnabas was a 'Jekyll and Hyde' character whose moments of cruelty were occasioned by his condition as a vampire. However, there was also some suggestion that Barnabas had always been prone to aggression, and that this had made him a willing victim to vampirism. In the series, Barnabas exhibits many of the traits of the classic vampire: he has super powers, including the ability to hypnotize subjects at will; he is very strong, enabling him to overpower his victims easily in a struggle; and he is able to change into a bat at any time. In addition, he is a sorcerer, and can appear and vanish in different places, or adopt strange voices and shapes so as to strike fear into onlookers.

The character of Barnabas Collins was introduced into the *Dark Shadows* series because ratings for the show were falling. The strategy certainly succeeded, and the show continued for five more years, with Collins becoming the undisputed star. In 1991, NBC revived the series, with Ben Cross in the role of Barnabas, a testament to the enduring appeal of the lovelorn vampire forever searching for his bride.

The *Dark Shadows* series also inspired a series of spin-off novels by Marilyn Ross. These were written by Canadian author Dan Ross, using his wife Marilyn's name. Ross was a writer for the Warner Paperback Library, who were contracted to produce a series of novels based on the show. Many of the storylines in the novel were original, but Ross used the characters in the show, especially that of Barnabas. According to Ross's widow Marilyn, he did not watch the TV shows, as he felt this would be confusing. Although Ross was the main writer, Marilyn also had a great deal of input; her particular skill was character development, while Ross's was the ability to write complex plots.

The series of novels had many fans. There were also four more novels in the series, written by Lara Parker, the actress who played Angelique in the series. To this day, there continues to be a cult following for the *Dark Shadows* series, which is regarded as something of a classic.

Jonathan Frid from the US TV series *Dark Shadows*.

Buffy the Vampire Slayer

The character of Buffy, an apparently ordinary 'valley girl' teenager who leads a double life as a vampire slayer, first appeared in the film *Buffy the Vampire Slayer*, released in 1992. Buffy, played by Kristy Swanson, is a cheerleading young woman who finds out that she has an important destiny, to kill vampires with her superhuman powers. The film, directed by Fran Rubel Kuzui and written by Joss Whedon, was a light-hearted send-up of the horror genre, and was moderately successful.

However, in an unusual twist, it was the more serious TV series of the same name, also written by Whedon, that proved to be more popular than the film. In the TV series, broadcast from 1997 to 2003, and starring Sarah Michelle Gellar, Whedon had more scope to explore deeper themes, using elements of the supernatural to stand as metaphors for the anxieties of teenagers and young adults. The show also attracted viewers because it emphasized the idea of young women as empowered: Buffy and her friends are strong, brave, clever individuals who use a number of resources to track down and destroy the vampires. This characterization of teenage girl was in marked contrast to most depictions of this age group and gender as airheaded, vain, and silly. For all these reasons, *Buffy the Vampire Slayer* quickly attracted a devoted following that appreciated its fresh, intelligent approach. And although, in many ways, it subverted the stereotypes of popular culture, it also celebrated the more positive aspects of TV drama, pairing up elements of the horror genre with a high-school narrative to provide an exciting new twist on a familiar theme.

The Forces of Darkness

The series follows the adventures of Buffy Summers, the newest Slayer. The mystical prophecy of the Slayer states that in each generation, only one girl in the whole world is 'the chosen one' and that 'she alone will wield the strength and skill to fight the vampires, demons and the forces of darkness; to stop the spread of their evil and the swell of their numbers.' It is Buffy's destiny to be the Slayer. She is guided and advised by her Watcher, who is a member of a secret organization that seeks to prepare the Slayer to fight these evil forces. In most of the episodes, a villain is defeated or prevented from doing harm, while a longer narrative plays out, often involving Buffy and her friends' relationships with each other. As the show progressed, the vampires they hunt are replaced by other creatures such as zombies, ghosts, and werewolves. In their quest to rid the world of evil, they use fighting skills, detective-style investigations, and research into ancient forms of folklore and mysticism.

In the first episodes of the series, Buffy moves to a new high school, Sunnydale, which happens to be built on top of a demon portal to another dimension, known as a Hellmouth. Her new school mates, Xander and Willow, help her to stop The Master, a powerful and very ancient vampire, from opening the Hellmouth and invading the school. In later episodes, other vampires appear and must be thwarted. Matters become more complicated when Buffy herself falls in love with a vampire, Angel, and sleeps with him. As a result, Angel, who has been given a human soul, loses his humanity and becomes a dangerous murderer. Buffy is forced to kill him, and although emotionally drained by this, she once again gathers her strength, and sets out on more adventures.

Buffy and Angel

Buffy, the main protagonist of the series, has extraordinary powers of physical and mental strength, including the ability to heal quickly and to intuit the motivations of others. Buffy only sleeps for a few hours due to the night being her busiest vampire slaying time. However, when she finally gets to rest she receives prophetic dreams that help with her fight against evil. She is guided by Rupert Giles, her Watcher, and helped by her friends, Willow and Xander. In the various narratives of the series, the thoughts and feelings of Buffy and her high-school friends are explored perceptively and with sensitivity.

The series inspired a spin-off, *Angel*, that was first broadcast in 1999. The story concerns Angel, a vampire who has a human soul, restored to him in revenge for a murder of a gypsy that he committed. His soul taunts him with guilt and remorse for his former crimes, and as a result he vows to battle evil in all its forms, though still prey to his own vampiric tendencies. Though darker in tone than *Buffy*, this show also proved very successful.

Sarah Michelle Gellar as
Buffy the Vampire Slayer

True Blood

True Blood, the HBO drama series about vampires, has become one of the most successful shows on today's TV screen. Intelligent, sexy, and fun, it uses the vampire myth to play with ideas about the relationship between ordinary, law-abiding members of society and those who are considered outcasts, offering the suggestion that 'supernatural creatures' such as vampires, telepaths, and shapeshifters, can now 'come out of the coffin' and 'mainstream' themselves into small-town human communities.

The series is based on *The Southern Vampire Mysteries* novels of Charlaine Harris. The story goes that TV writer Alan Ball (who had previously worked on HBO's *Six Feet Under*) was waiting for a dental appointment, and whiled away the time by leafing through *Dead Until Dark*, the first of the books, at Barnes and Noble. He was captivated, and when he brought the idea to the TV company, they gave him the go-ahead.

The drama is set in a conservative small Louisiana town where hatred of vampires is rife (there's a motel sign saying 'God Hates Fangs' in the opening credits) and those who tolerate them are referred to as 'fang bangers'. We follow the adventures of waitress Sookie Stackhouse (Anna Paquin) at Merlotte's Bar & Grill, a local hang-out for ne'er-do-wells. Unbeknown to her customers, Sookie is telepathic and can read their thoughts. However, when a handsome stranger called Bill Compton (Stephen Moyer) walks in, she finds she can't tap in to his mind. As it turns out, that's because he's a vampire; but even when she realizes he's 173 years old, she can't help falling for him. When the sleepy town is rocked by a series of mysterious murders, Sookie begins to encounter the world of vampires, learning that they live on synthetic blood, called TruBlood, invented by Japanese scientists and sold in convenience stores. She also runs in to humans addicted to vampire blood, who are prepared to kill to get their fix. The message is, of course, a liberal, humanist one: that the distinctions between 'normal' individuals and misfits are never simple, and that vampires/outcasts can be victims, too. To date, the show has attracted over 12 million viewers per week, becoming HBO's most watched series since *The Sopranos*.

ABOVE AND RIGHT: Characters from HBO's drama series *True Blood*

Vampire Movies

Nosferatu

Directed by F.W. Murnau, 1922. Starring Max Schreck. This adaptation of Bram Stoker's *Dracula* was not released at the time owing to a dispute between Murnau and Stoker's widow over copyright. But bootleg copies of the film survived, and it has since become a classic, with a famously chilling performance by Schreck as the rat-like Count Dracula.

Dracula

Directed by Tod Browning, 1931. Starring Bela Lugosi, Helen Chandler, David Manners, Edward Van Sloan. Based on the stage adaptation of the novel, this highly publicized movie introduced cinema audiences to Bela Lugosi in the title role. His menacing performance had audiences fainting in the aisles, and the film proved a massive box-office success.

Vampyr

Directed by Carl Theodor Dreyer, 1932. Starring Julian West, Maurice Schutz, Sybille Schmitz. A slow-paced but hallucinogenic take on the vampire myth, in which vampires lure villagers to commit suicide, then becoming servants of the devil. Panned on its release, the movie is now viewed as a groundbreaking piece of film history.

Horror of Dracula

Directed by Terence Fisher, 1958. Starring Christopher Lee, Peter Cushing, John Van Eyssen. Known in the UK as *Dracula*, this film was made on a low budget but went on to break box-office records. It also spawned eight follow-ups, which were dubbed 'Hammer Horrors' after the studio that made them.

The Last Man on Earth

Directed by Ubaldo Ragona and Sidney Salkow, 1964. Starring Vincent Price. Based on the Richard Matheson novel *I Am Legend*, this picture was filmed in Rome, Italy. Although Matheson described the result as disappointing, the film has since won admirers, and currently has a sizeable cult following.

Blood for Dracula

Directed by Paul Morrissey, 1974. Starring Udo Kier, Joe Dallesandro, Maxime McKendry, Stefania Casini. Made by the Andy Warhol stable, this is essentially a spoof, but it has a love of the Hollywood horror genre at its heart, and in some ways is a requiem for it. Also features a cameo appearance by Roman Polanski.

Martin

Directed by George A. Romero, 1977. Starring John Amplas. Made by the director of the seminal *Living Dead* zombie series, *Martin* is considered to be one of the best B movie horror films of the seventies. The film was made on a low budget, in real locations, with friends and family of the director in supporting roles.

Rabid

Directed by David Cronenberg, 1977. Starring Marilyn Chambers, Frank Moore, Robert A. Silverman. This 'body horror' movie tells the story of a woman who grows a phallic organ under her armpit and goes on to suck blood through it, infecting others with a form of rabies and causing widespread chaos.

Nosferatu the Vampyre

Directed by Werner Herzog, 1979. Starring Klaus Kinski, Isabelle Adjani, Bruno Ganz, Roland Topor. Herzog considered Murnau's 1922 classic the best film ever to come out of West Germany, and conceived this as a remake. It was warmly praised by the critics but did not prove so popular with cinema goers.

The Hunger

Directed by Tony Scott, 1983. Starring Susan Sarandon, Catherine Deneuve, David Bowie. Adapted from the novel by Whitley Strieber, Scott's debut feature was praised for its atmospherics, but criticized as slow-moving and badly plotted. However, its dark glamour and lush visuals earned it a cult following, especially among denizens of the goth subculture.

Near Dark

Directed by Kathryn Bigelow, 1987. Starring Adrian Pasdar, Jenny Wright. Cleverly mixing vampires with elements of the Western and biker movie genres, this was one of a number of movies released in the eighties that picked up some of the more serious themes in vampire mythology. A cult classic.

The Lost Boys

Directed by Joel Schumacher, 1987. Starring Jason Patric, Corey Haim, Kiefer Sutherland. With a title referencing the 'lost boys' of J.M. Barrie's *Peter Pan*, the film tells the story of two young men from Arizona who move to California and find themselves embroiled in conflict with a gang of teenage vampires.

Dracula

Directed by Francis Ford Coppola, 1992. Starring Gary Oldman, Winona Ryder, Anthony Hopkins, Keanu Reeves. 'Big names, a big budget, big sets, a big, thundering score and even big hair' was how one critic described this film. He went on to pan it, but audiences loved it, and it was a box-office smash.

Interview with the Vampire

Directed by Neil Jordan, 1994. Starring Tom Cruise, Brad Pitt, Antonio Banderas, Kirsten Dunst. Based on the Anne Rice Chronicles, the movie initially attracted controversy because of its violence, and the fact that Rice was not enthusiastic about the casting of Cruise in the role of Lestat. However, it ultimately went on to be a hit.

From Dusk till Dawn

Directed by Robert Rodriguez, 1996. Starring Harvey Keitel, George Clooney, Quentin Tarantino, Juliet Lewis, Salma Hayek. A pulp B-movie extravaganza, full of trashy sex, violence, and gore, one critic commented: 'I can think of worse things to sit through than an orgy of bullets, exploding corpses and stripper vampires'.

Blade

Directed by Stephen Norrington, 1998. Starring Wesley Snipes, Stephen Dorff. Snipes plays Blade, a character based on the fictional hero of Marvel Comics fame. Blade is half human, half vampire, and fights off a vampire invasion. The film was a massive box-office success, ushering a revival of the American superhero movie, and spawning two sequels.

Dracula: Pages from a Virgin's Diary

Directed by Guy Maddin 2002. Starring Zhang Wei-Qiang, Tara Birtwhistle, David Moroni. This silent film, initially destined for limited release only, won many admirers for its originality. Based on the Royal Winnipeg Ballet's interpretation of Bram Stoker's *Dracula*, it takes the familiar vampire story and transforms it into a dream-like sequence.

Underworld

Directed by Len Wiseman, 2003. Starring Kate Beckinsale, Scott Speedman. The tale of a female vampire who hunts Lycans or werewolves, the film was negatively received in general, the consensus being that it was over-styled and overacted, without rising to the level of enjoyable shlock. However, it went on to spawn two sequels.

Let the Right One In

Directed by Tomas Alfredson, 2008.
Starring Kare Hedebrant, Lina
Leandersson, Per Ragnar. Set in the suburbs
of Stockholm, this heartwarming story of
a 12-year-old boy who befriends a vampire
child was a surprise hit, garnering many
awards. The screenplay was written by
novelist John Ajvide Lindqvist, based on his
book of the same name.

Twilight

Directed by Catherine Hardwicke, 2008.
Starring Kristen Stewart, Robert Pattinson.
Some felt that the movie adaptation had
lost some of the 'bite' of Stephenie Meyer's
novel, a love story between a human girl
and a vampire boy. However, the film's two
young leads were generally praised, described
as 'sizzling like two sausages in a pan'.

Kiefer Sutherland

Kiefer Sutherland (above) starred as
a teenage vampire in *The Lost Boys*
(1987) directed by Joel Schumacher.
He was praised for his performance as
the wild leader of a motorcycle gang
who turns out to be heading a posse of
murderous vampires. 'No one sneers
with more conviction' commented the
New York Times.

Vampires in Pop

Rock'n'roll has, from its earliest days, borrowed elements from the horror genre, and the vampire myth is no exception. Artists such as Screamin' Jay Hawkins, Alice Cooper, Marilyn Manson and Ozzy Osbourne are among those who have brought a strong gothic aesthetic of graveyard gore into the world of pop. In doing so, they have loyally upheld the crucial rock tradition of disgusting and horrifying the establishment, whether identified as government officials, social commentators, or parental figures.

Freak and horror shows

On the whole, the antics of the 'vampires of pop' have been fairly harmless, designed to entertain rather than to incite violence. Their vaudevillian stage routines have had an element of humour to them, often being performed tongue-in-cheek, but that has not stopped the authorities and the media from constantly voicing their anxieties about their corrupting effect on the youth of today. In particular, politicians and social commentators focus on the violence of the stage shows, and the effect this may have on impressionable children and teenagers, often ignoring the fact that such antics have a strong element of parody about them, and that freak and horror shows of one type or another are nothing new. Indeed, they have been going on since medieval times, when travelling fairs would exhibit freaks of nature, whether human or animal, and from the Victorian period, when a morbid fascination for such curiosities was at its height.

Despite, or perhaps because of the perennial censure that they have encountered, the 'vampires' of pop have continued in their mission to bring the most sensational elements of the horror genre into the centre of contemporary music, whether it be heavy metal, garage, punk, or even hip hop; and, in the future, this fruitful partnership of horror and noise that so appeals to adolescents, young adults, and certain older sections of the listening public, looks set to continue.

Screamin' Jay Hawkins

The pairing of gothic horror with rock'n'roll has been a long, respected tradition since the fifties. Borrowing from the carnivals, vaudeville tents, medicine men, freak shows, and travelling fairs that were so much a part of entertainment for ordinary working people across America in the late nineteenth and early twentieth century, in the post-war period a number of black performers began to introduce these elements into rock'n'roll.

One of the first to do so was one Jalacy Hawkins, a musician, singer and actor with a wildly – some would say absurdly – theatrical show. Born in Cleveland, Ohio, in 1929, Hawkins initially studied piano, and hoped to become a serious singer in the style of Paul Robeson. However, his dreams, like those of so many talented black musicians, were dashed, and during World War II, he ended up entertaining the troops as a blues singer. He also became Middleweight Boxing Champion for Alaska.

In 1956, changing his name to Screamin' Jay Hawkins, he recorded his hit single, *I Put A Spell on You*. Originally intended to be a gentle, sweet ballad, it turned out rather differently. Legend has it that during the recording session, the entire band were blind drunk, Hawkins particularly so. What emerged was a raw slice of guttural rock'n'roll, and after somehow grunting and howling his way through the song, Hawkins passed out. Later, when it became a hit, he was forced to relearn it so that he could perform it on stage.

Much to general surprise, the song became an early rock'n'roll hit, and Hawkins was soon performing it to hordes of screaming teenagers. To entertain his young audience, Hawkins dressed in an outlandish gold and leopard-skin costume, often with a flowing cape. He also borrowed from voodoo, using props such as a skull on a stick and rubber snakes. It is thought that emerging from a coffin on stage was DJ and promoter Alan Freed's idea, and that Hawkins was paid to do the stunt. Be that as it may, the sight of this bizarrely dressed man jumping out of a coffin on a smoke-filled stage had the desired effect, and Hawkins continued with this stage act for the rest of his career, long after the popularity of his records had ceased.

Screamin' Jay Hawkins

Alice Cooper

Hawkins' 'vampire and voodoo' stage act was a big influence on several later rock acts, including Alice Cooper. Born Vincent Furnier in Detroit, Michigan, in 1948, he formed a band called The Earwigs while still in high school, but later, after several changes of line-up, altered the name to Alice Cooper. This name was said to have come to him in a session with an ouija board, in which he made contact with a seventeenth century witch called Alice Cooper. Later, Cooper admitted that this

Alice Cooper on stage in 1980.

was a publicity stunt, and that he actually chose the name because it 'sounded like a cute little girl with a hatchet behind her back'. However, the name proved to be an essential factor in Cooper's success; initially, it was only used as a band name, but after fans started to refer to the band's leader as 'Alice', Cooper decided to use the name himself, also dressing appropriately in an androgynous style, which further alienated his critics.

Eating a live chicken

As the band's career progressed, Cooper soon showed himself to be aware of the value of publicity, especially bad publicity, and began to use it to great effect. In 1969, while performing in Toronto, a chicken wandered on to the stage – the reasons for this are still unknown. Without hesitation, Cooper picked it up and tossed it into the auditorium, believing that chickens were able to fly. Instead, it dropped down into the crowd, who apparently tore it to pieces. The next day, it was reported in the press that Cooper had bitten the head off the chicken and had even gone so far as to drink its blood on stage. He immediately denied the report, but after a conversation with his producer, Frank Zappa, allowed it to circulate, realizing the potential that such publicity had to increase the shock value of his stage act. The notion that he was a vampire, who lived on the blood of animals, was one that he began to encourage, living up to his deathly reputation by wearing streaks of dark make-up around his eyes, and dressing in black.

It was not long before Cooper's live show began to feature other elements derived

A GUILLOTINE, COMPLETE WITH EXECUTIONER

from the horror genre, such as a real boa constrictor, which he often wrapped around his neck, an electric chair, and a gallows. In his shows, he would perform such antics as the chopping up of bloodied baby dolls, much to the consternation of his many horrified critics.

The executioner

The band's single 'School's Out' reached the top ten in 1972, selling over a million copies. The following year their album *Billion Dollar Babies* reached the number one slot in both the US and the UK, and their reputation was sealed. Alice Cooper began to tour more intensively, and the shows became wilder, featuring all kinds of gruesome effects, from extracted dancing teeth to a guillotine, complete with executioner. Not surprisingly, the establishment were outraged, and political figures and social commentators clamoured to have them banned from performing. This, of course, only increased their popularity.

In the years that followed, the constant touring took its toll on Cooper, who became an alcoholic. He formed a drinking club with his friends known as The Hollywood Vampires, but after a run of accidents and mishaps, some of them on stage, decided to quit drinking and become a born-again Christian. Thankfully, however, he has refrained from lecturing his many fans on the evil of his former ways, restricting himself to the observation that his enjoyment of golf was a great help to him in his rehabilitation.

Marilyn Manson

Today, gothic horror has become a staple of rock music, especially heavy metal. One of the foremost exponents of the vampire tradition is Marilyn Manson, who has continued Alice Cooper's mission to irritate the establishment, horrifying social commentators with his gruesome appearance and outrageous stage shows. In particular, he has perfected an eerie 'just popped up from the grave' style of dress and make-up, using modern theatrical techniques. These include a special contact lens that looks like a wall eye. (Similar contact lenses, called 'The Marilyn Manson Look' are apparently now available in shops.) Legend has it that Manson also has a large collection of prosthetic limbs and that his prized sartorial possession is a jacket made from the skin of conjoined twin lambs.

In recent years, Manson has switched his attention from music to film and art, though his artworks have not to date met with great critical acclaim. However, like Alice Cooper before him, he continues to be a thorn in the side of the authorities, and off stage comes over as a witty figure whose aim, as well as to shock, is to encourage tolerance for the more unconventional and excluded individuals in our society – a reading of the vampire myth that has become central to fiction, film, and pop in recent years. He often, in his public pronouncements, pokes fun at the hypocrisy of the establishment, the falseness of show business, and social snobbery, with remarks such as, 'In the end we're all Springer guests, really, we just haven't been on the show', and, 'The ability to make small children cry at the grocery store I like better than the fame.'

Ozzy Osbourne

Another man who is synonymous with shock tactics is Ozzy Osbourne. When he first embarked on a solo career he went to meet the staff at his record label. Bizarrely, he decided to release some doves into the air to attract attention to himself, presumably to make a memorable entrance. However, as he did this, no one noticed and instead he grabbed a dove and bit its head off. As he spat the head out a security guard approached him and escorted him outside, leaving a bloody trail as he went. This wasn't the last time he'd use an animal to get noticed; in 1982 Ozzy shocked his audience during a gig when he appeared to bite the head off a live bat. Since the incident there has been much debate over whether the bat was alive or dead. According to *Rolling Stone* magazine the bat was alive, but the fan who actually launched the creature onstage claimed the bat was dead. Ozzy later stated that he believed the bat to be a toy as it was completely still and that's why he'd jokingly put it in his mouth. However, its wings started to flap and it bit him as he tried to remove it from his mouth, unfortunately he somehow ripped its head off in the process.

Allegedly Ozzy later received anti-rabies injections and concluded the bat must have been petrified by the stage lights and that's why it looked so toy-like.

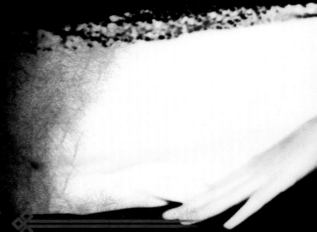

Heavy metal singer Ozzy Osbourne stands laughing
over a woman chained to a table, circa 1982

Glossary

Apotropaic – a method of warding off a vampire, such as hanging up garlic, sprinkling holy water over a grave, etc. Such rituals and objects, believed to have magical properties, were common in the Middle Ages.

Aristocratic vampire – the idea of the vampire as refined aristocrat derives from early nineteenth-century gothic literature. It was first introduced in John Polidori's The Vampyre (1813). Prior to this time, vampires were thought of as monstrously ugly.

Aswang – a creature from Filipino folklore who is said to turn from a pretty girl by day into an evil, bloodsucking old crone at night, growing bat-like wings and a long tongue.

Baptism – Christian baptism was thought to help prevent a baby from becoming a vampire in later life, and was thus seen as an immediate necessity for protecting newborns.

Burial rites – observing the proper Christian rituals for burial was considered crucial in ensuring that corpses did not become vampires after being interred. People who met with accidents, whose bodies were not buried, were thought to be at risk of becoming vampires.

Caul – a child born in a membrane from the amniotic sac was sometimes thought, in early times, to be a vampire. Alternatively, the child might be seen as protected from harm, especially from drowning.

Chupacabra – the 'goat sucker' is a creature still feared in Mexico and Puerto Rico, who is said to attack live cattle. Recent sightings were reported in the 1990s, leading to mass hysteria.

Cihuateteo – in Aztec mythology, the evil spirit of a woman who has died in childbirth, and haunts crossroads, waiting to steal children and seduce men.

Consumption – otherwise known as tuberculosis, the symptoms of this contagious disease (coughing up blood, becoming thin, pale, weak, etc.) were attributed to vampirism in early times.

Crucifix – traditionally, the crucifix, or even a simple cross, was thought to function as a powerful deterrent, or apotropaic to vampires, causing them to weaken and run away.

Decapitation – the severing of the head from the body. In medieval times, corpses were sometimes decapitated in the belief that this would prevent the dead person from becoming a vampire.

Decomposition – misinterpretation of the natural process of a corpse's decomposition (bloating, blood running from orifices, etc.) was a powerful factor in the creation of the vampire myth in the medieval era.

'Double faith' – the holding of pagan as well as Christian beliefs, often in a contradictory way, as happened in medieval Slavic countries, where the vampire myth first arose.

Draculin – a substance in bat saliva that acts as an anti-coagulant, stopping the blood of a victim clotting so that the bat can drink it. Named after Count Dracula.

Exhumation – the practice of digging up dead bodies, in this case to see if they had transformed into vampires.

Exorcism – various methods used to drive out evil spirits, ghosts, vampires, and other revenants, often through using Christian prayer, imagery, symbols, etc.

Fangs – in medieval times, people with long incisors were feared as vampires, and this feature went on to become a central part of vampire lore, especially celebrated in film.

Garlic – since vampires are said to have a strong sense of smell, hanging garlic over a doorway or fireplace was thought to deter them.

Gothic – in literature, a style of writing focussing on the supernatural, grotesque, and gloomy, dating from the eighteenth century.

Hammer horror – the Hammer Horrors were a series of low-budget British movies, names after their studio Hammer Film Productions. The first of which was released in 1958 and starred Christopher Lee as Dracula.

Hawthorn – commonly known as May, or mayblossom, the hawthorn is believed in Slavic folklore to be fatal to vampires. Corpses were often buried with a sprig of hawthorn in the coffin.

Heat sensors – vampire bats have heat sensors that allow them to sense blood near the surface of the victim's skin, for example, in the neck.

Haematophagy – the state of deriving nourishment solely from a diet of blood. Examples of animals who feed in this way include vampire bats, worms, nematodes, leeches, and lampreys.

Holy water – sprinkling consecrated water over a grave or doorway was said to deter vampires from exiting or entering.

Hydrophobia – fear of water. The vampire's alleged fear of water may be related to the behaviour of people suffering from rabies, who often experience intense terror of water as part of their madness.

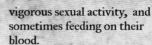

Impalement – the practise of piercing bodies, dead or alive, with a large stake. Vlad Dracul, the medieval Romanian prince on whom the legend of Dracula was partly based, is thought to have murdered thousands of victims in this way.

Lamia – a female demon from Ancient Greek mythology, who preys on small children at night, especially newborns, carrying them off and devouring them in revenge for the murder of her own children.

Medieval vampire – in contrast to the suave aristocrat of gothic literature, the vampire of the medieval imagination was seen as a hideous, vile-smelling revenant. It was memorably described as 'an enormous corpulence' by one medieval commentator.

Mind control – the ability to assert control over others through psychological means rather than force. Vampires are sometimes said to have this ability.

Mirror image – vampires are believed to have no reflection when standing in front of a mirror.

Mutilation – dismemberment of a body. In medieval times, corpses were sometimes buried with head, hands, and feet cut off to prevent them rising from the grave.

Nail – a large iron nail driven into the head was thought to stop a corpse from becoming a vampire.

Nosferatu – meaning 'the plague bringer', this type of vampire dates from the medieval era, in which the vampire was seen as a hideous creature who would spread disease and pestilence among the community.

'Old religion' – a set of ancient pagan beliefs held by Slavic nations, and persisting after the introduction of Christianity. Amongst these beliefs is a fear of vampires.

Penny dreadful – serial stories of the Victorian era, appearing in cheap editions and appealing to teenagers and young adults. The popular story Varney the Vampire first appeared here.

Plague – any of a number of contagious diseases bringing death and destruction to whole communities. In early times, vampires were feared as causing plagues, hence the term 'Nosferatu' (see above).

Porphyria – a largely congenital disease which can cause reddening of the teeth and nails, as well as light sensitivity, giving rise to the suspicion that the sufferer is a vampire.

Revenant – a spirit returning from the grave in human form, such as a ghost, vampire, or other supernatural creature. Sometimes these spirits are viewed sympathetically, as sad, lonely beings condemned to 'eternal death', but more often they are feared as harmful, returning from the grave to wreak their revenge on the living.

Rosewood – a stake (see below) made of rosewood or ash was traditionally thought to be doubly effective in ensuring the permanent dispatch of a vampire.

Seventh son – according to ancient Slavic folklore, the seventh child in a family was often suspected of being a vampire. If the child's older siblings were all the same sex, this was seen as more likely to be the case.

Silver – in some cultures, silver is believed to be lethal to vampires. A live vampire who is impervious to ordinary bullets may be shot by a silver one, and silver nails driven into a coffin may prevent a vampire's escape.

Stake – running a stake through the heart of a corpse was thought, in medieval times, to ensure that it would not come to life as a vampire. This was also said to be an effective way of killing a live vampire.

Succubus – a vampire-like female creature of medieval folklore, the succubus seduces men, draining them of strength through vigorous sexual activity, and sometimes feeding on their blood.

Sunlight – early accounts of vampirism contain no allusion to the idea that vampires are afraid of sunlight. This appears to be a late addition to vampire lore, especially popular in film.

Transubstantiation – in the Christian religion, the idea that the bread and wine in the celebration of Mass literally become the body and blood of Christ, which is then eaten and drunk by the celebrants.

Upir – the first written occurrence of the word 'vampire'. The word appeared as a scribbled note in the manuscript of an eleventh-century Book of Psalms, translated by an unknown priest for a Novgorodian Prince.

Vampire – Today, the word 'vampire' is defined variously as 'a corpse that rises nightly from its grave to drink the blood of the living' and as 'a mythical creature which overcomes death by sucking the blood from living humans'.

Vampire bat – the common vampire bat, which feeds mostly on animals, is found in Latin America. Its relatives include other bloodsucking bats, including the white-winged vampire bat, and the hairy legged vampire bat.

Varkolak – one of a number of undead revenant creatures occurring in Bulgarian folklore. These may include evil spirits, vampires and werewolves.

Werewolf – a close associate of the vampire, the werewolf also derives from medieval folklore. Werewolves are thought to be human beings who have changed their shape, either of their own volition or as a form of punishment for an earlier wrongdoing.

Wild rose – the wild rose is believed in many cultures to have magical properties, among them the ability to ward off vampires.

Index

© 2010 Oxford Publishing Ventures Ltd

This edition published in 2019 by Chartwell Books
an imprint of The Quarto Group
142 West 36th Street, 4th Floor
New York, New York 10001
New York, NY 10018, USA
T (212) 779-4972 **F** (212) 779-6058
www.QuartoKnows.com

Chartwell Books titles are also available at discount for retail, wholesale, promotional, and bulk purchase. For details, contact the Special Sales Manager by email at specialsales@quarto.com or by mail at The Quarto Group, Attn: Special Sales Manager, 100 Cummings Center Suite 265D, Beverly, MA 01915, USA.

ISBN-13: 978-0-7858-3741-1

10 9 8 7 6 5 4 3 2 1

Printed in China

Picture Credits